Н

Tamara Bris

How to Recover From Emotional Abuse: Heal Your Broken Heart

© Copyright by Tamara Bris 2013.

First edition

All rights reserved.

ISBN 978-1494288730

All rights reserved under International Copyright Law.

No part of this book may be stored or reproduced in any form without the express written permission of the copyright holder.

* * * * * * * * * * * *

This book may contain references to specific commercial products, process or service by trade name, trademark, manufacturer, or otherwise, specific brand-name products and/or trade names of products, which are trademarks or registered trademarks and/or trade names, and these are property of their respective owners. Tamara Bris, her publishers and associates have no association with any specific commercial products, process or service by trade name, trademark, manufacturer, or otherwise, specific brand-name products and/or trade names of products.

Legal Disclaimer

This book is designed to provide information and motivation to our readers. It is sold with the understanding that the author is not engaged to render any type of psychological, legal, or any other kind of professional advice. The content is the sole expression and opinion of its author. No warranties or guarantees are expressed or implied by the contents of this book. The author shall not be liable for any physical, psychological, emotional, financial, or commercial damages, including, but not limited to, special, incidental, consequential or other damages. Our views and rights are the same: You are responsible for your own choices, actions, and results.

Table of Contents

Introduction…………………………………….9

Chapter 1. What is emotional abuse?................19

It's all about the power

It began so well

Unreasonable expectations

Unpredictable temper

The silent treatment

Technical definition of emotional abuse

Five kinds of abuse

Why do I feel a bond with him and want to go back?

Chapter 2. DING, DONG – Warning Signs…35

The abuser

The victim

Chapter 3. My personal story of Abuse……....53

Chapter 4. Victim's stories of Abuse ………….67

Chapter 5. Profile of the typical Abuser………79

What caused them to be like this?

Biological reasons for abuse

Social causes

You can't help your abuser

Chapter 6. Profile of the typical victim………..89

Social Causes

Abused people have the following in common

Once someone experiences a toxic relationship why are they more likely to repeat the pattern?

How do you approach relationships?

Chapter 7. Why don't you just leave?...............101

Chapter 8. Why do so many victims return to their abuser?..109

How to deal with your ex once you have left

Chapter 9. The Healing Process……………...119

Loneliness

Grief

Anger

Depression

Forgiveness

Therapy

Look for the lesson. – Learn from your experience

Chapter 10. Build your confidence and self-esteem…………………………………………….133

How do I look?

I accept myself

Love yourself

Mirror work

Take the focus off yourself

Confidence building ideas

Do feel good things

Chapter 11. Kick-start your New Life……….143

Change your thoughts

The law of attraction – 'like attracts like'

Positive thoughts

Visualization

Meditation

Keep a journal

Chapter 12. Dating after abuse – avoid the pitfalls………………………..……………….157

What happened at the beginning?

Change your old patterns

My ideal partner

My relationship bill of rights

Deal-breakers – Boundaries

What does a healthy relationship look like?

Chapter 13. What the Research Says about Emotional Abuse..................................173

Did you suffer emotional abuse as a Child?

Chapter 14. Conclusion...................…..............181

Where to get help.....................………......186

Recommended Reading..........................187

Bibliography................….....................191

Introduction.

My name is Tamara Bris, and I've been a victim of emotional and verbal abuse.

My first husband was both verbally and emotionally abusive to me and controlled me through fear and manipulation. He went so far as to use guilt in order to get me to marrying him. I know that's hard to believe, but it's true.

Even though we were severely mismatched and the marriage was miserable, I stayed for quite some years because I felt I *should,* because I had committed to it.

My pattern of abuse had begun a long time before my first marriage. I was brought up in a very strict and controlling cult-like religion. The religion had controlled me through fear. I suppose it was fear of not doing the '*right thing*' - fear of going to hell. The rules were strict, and not following them was not even a consideration.

When I married my husband, I saw no other option but to be married to somebody from the same religion. As in all cults, marriages stay within the cult community.

After I came to my senses and left the religion and my first husband, I dated a lot of different guys over the next three years, but no one held my interest longer than a couple of months. That changed when I met 'John' (this is not his real name, which has been omitted for legal reasons). It was my relationship with John that was the most traumatic relationship of my life. I share the details of our relationship in Chapter 3.

The relationship with John lasted fifteen years. After I left him I was at the lowest point in my life. I wasn't in love with my first husband - so leaving him had felt great - but I had been very much in love with John and I was hurting severely. As I was trying to rebuild my life it occurred to me that I was in a pattern of abuse - From the cult, my parents, my first husband, and then John. Why? Why did it keep happening in my life over and over again?

I realized I was the common denominator in all these situations, so the answer must lay within me. Somehow I was attracting these abusive people towards myself. It became clear that I had to be thinking and acting like a victim, but in what ways? How can I think differently, how can I react differently to things people say and do, other than in the way I've been programmed?

As I write this I'm still amazed at how I had let other people control me for so many years, since I've always thought of myself as intelligent and independent. Obviously, I was swayed too much by what other people wanted and expected of me. I had become a 'people pleaser' -putting what *I* wanted last. Not only that – I didn't even *know* what I wanted or needed. I had lost myself.

I had to break this ingrained pattern because I never wanted to feel the way that John made me feel again. I felt like I was trapped in a web of trying to gain his approval. I wanted to break free of the dark cloud hanging over me and get rid of my negative patterns for good.

I knew I deserved better. I set out on a mission to **re-program** my mind, create the right mindset and undo the negative patterns of the past forty plus years.

This book is designed to help people who are going through what I went through. Hopefully, the things I learnt along the way will be able to help you gain back control of your life too.

* * *

Why is he doing this to me? How can he do this to me if he says he loves me? Your inner world is in turmoil. You feel like you are drowning - or suffocating - and the one you love is looking the other way, cold and uncaring. Words alone cannot express how damaging emotional abuse is to a person. Neither can words describe the feeling of frustration and helplessness that the abused person feels deep down in their soul.

Note: For convenience and because the research suggests that the majority of abusers are men, throughout this book I refer to the abuser as "he" and the victim as "she." In many cases it is the men who are abused. I write as if relationships are heterosexual however, same-sex relationships may also be abusive.

What is emotional abuse?

Emotional abuse is about power and control. One partner wields the power over the other. However, emotional abuse can be more subtle than the other forms of abuse. It can include sulking, withholding approval, attention or affection. Very often one partner controls the other's important decisions, most often regarding money. It can even go so far as to involve controlling what their partner wears or the way they have their hair cut or styled.

Typically, the victim reports that the person who abuses (the abuser) twists their words, controls the finances, has temper tantrums and tells lies. Their behavior alternates between charming and offensive and is often described as 'Jekyll and Hyde.'

The abuser arranges the timing of their abuse to catch the victim off guard. The shocked and dismayed victim can't figure out what triggered their abuser's ghastly behavior. Their controlling, manipulating ways leave the victim feeling degraded, hurt, scared, inferior and isolated.

The victim of such abuse finds that their life slowly erodes to the point that they are living the life that their abuser projects on to them. Some victims have changed their core beliefs and attitudes in order to comply with their abuser's beliefs. Of course, as the abuser is the dominating force in this relationship, the victim would dare not make a decision without the approval of her abuser.

How do I get my life back after abuse?

There's a lot of misguided, bad and generally misleading information to be found in published material, on or offline. For example, 'forget about it and move on,' or 'put it behind you, it's over.'

Anyone who's been through emotional abuse knows the deep pain felt by such abuse. You can't just 'forget about it' and it's not that easy to 'just put it behind you.'

I felt I was going mad. One minute I'd miss him and want to go back to him and then the next minute I hated him for how he had treated me. So why did I feel like going back to him? What was this contradictory feeling that we belonged together?

Why do I feel like I want to go back to him?

This is the thing that I personally hate to admit, but it's very common in abusive relationships – *after I left I often thought about going back*!!

I know I'm not alone though. Before I was in one of these relationships, I would see battered women on television who would go back to the men who had hit them. I couldn't for the life of me understand why they would possibly go back. It really doesn't make any sense. That is until I found out about a phenomenon called 'trauma bonding.' This bonding occurs when abuse is intermittent and unexpected and terrifies the victim so much that their mind goes into a type of survival mode, which causes them to develop strong feelings of love and connection or bonding, to the person who is abusing them. I explain this fully in Chapter 7.

Realizing I wasn't in love with my abuser and that I was a victim of trauma bonding helped me to recover. My head knew I couldn't be in the relationship, but my heart – that was a different story.

Often times however, verbal and emotional abuse *are* forerunners to physical abuse. In my experience, which started as verbal and emotional abuse, it started to border on physical abuse (which would appear to be an 'accident').

FACT: If you have been in one abusive relationship you are very likely to end up in

another one. It is important that you know the answers to the following questions to avoid further abusers.

* How did I become a victim in the first place?
* What are the warning signs of emotional abuse?
* How do I establish boundaries to avoid abuse?
* How do I recognize when I'm being abused?
* How could this have happened to me?
* I'm a strong independent woman why didn't I leave at the first sign of abuse?
* Why did I constantly make excuses?
* Why do I miss him and want to go back to him?

What now? Okay, I'm assuming you are out of the relationship if you are reading this book, so what now?

* How do you begin to find that person you used to be?
* How do you even begin to pick up the broken pieces of your life?

* How do I heal my broken heart?
* How do I be happy again?

I hope you find this book useful in your journey back to *you*!

Chapter 1. What is emotional abuse?

'Oh no, it's nothing like *your* situation,' Karen said, 'we really get on well together. You don't understand what it's like. We really connect on a deep level, both of us have never felt like this before," she paused, and then continued, "He tells me that I make him want to be a better person."

Karen had phoned me twice when she was upset about the way her new boyfriend spoke to her and the horrible, hurtful things he had said to her. I tried to tell her that it was emotional abuse and she wouldn't hear of it. She did go on to admit that she feels like she can't have an opinion and he *shuts her down* if she tries to talk about certain things. He also threatens to leave her.

What my friend doesn't understand is that abusive relationships *are* wonderful, even spectacular a good percentage of the time. These men aren't abusive 100% of the time. These men can also be your best friend, and can be kind, caring and even loving. Karen is experiencing the highs and lows, the roller coaster pattern of an abusive relationship. However, all she can say over and over is, 'I've never felt like this before.' Because she *feels* the highs of the love and the connection with this man she can't see that he is acting in abusive ways to her at times. She wants so much to make it work that she is in denial.

IT'S ALL ABOUT THE POWER

Emotional abuse is all about power and the control they have which comes with this power. The abuser attains the power in the relationship by lying, manipulating and eroding all the confidence and self-esteem of the victim. The victim's every move is monitored and then criticized. The victim would dare not make a decision without consulting the abuser.

The victim, having lost confidence and the ability to think clearly, ends up handing all their power over to their abuser. The relationship is out of balance and resembles more of a parent-child relationship rather than a partnership, where both members share equality.

In Karen's case – she is a lawyer with a high-profile law firm, she is intelligent and she is beautiful, yet she says things to me like, 'I can't see why Jerome would like me, he can have any woman he wants,' and 'women are chasing him all the time and yet he is with me.' She wonders why her new man is with her and seems to think that he is the only man in the world for her. She doesn't see how wonderful *she* is. She could have anyone that *she* wants. I tell her that constantly, she agrees with me, but obviously doesn't acknowledge it on a deeper level.

I haven't met Jerome yet, but from what she has told me he seems to know that she is crazy about him and he is using that knowledge to torture and control her. He threatens to leave and taunts her by saying that he might go out with someone else, to the point she ends up in tears. The fact that Karen is financially independent and gorgeous looking is irrelevant to her handing her emotional power over to this man.

From an outsider looking in, it really is amazing that Karen is in denial about Jerome's behavior. Especially when she is aware of everything I went through with John. She says it's not the same, even though he is making her feel the way that John had made me feel, 'not good enough.'

IT BEGAN SO WELL

Felicia 31, Cairns
It started out so nice and romantic. He paid for trips away together; he always gave me flowers and even expensive jewelry. Then things started to change. He always had to know where I was and he demanded I stop going out with my friends. Arguments would often end with him disappearing without telling me where he was going. I think he did that just to be cruel because he knew I would worry about where he was.

No one would ever willingly enter into abusive relationships. The trap is that they don't look like abusive relationships at the start; neither do these loving men look like abusers. These relationships, like most relationships, start off really well.

Abusive relationships often begin with the abuser sweeping the victim off her feet and sometimes the abuser may even want to get very serious way too quickly. The victim thinks she is the luckiest girl in the world and she convinces herself that she has found 'the one,' 'the man of her dreams.' From thereon she is committed to making the relationship with this wonderful man work. She daydreams that the relationship will last forever. Together, they talk about the future and even build long-term plans.

Once the victim feels safe, secure and settled in the relationship she notices things are not quite right. Some subtle small things will occur, but typically there will be a major burst of temper and aggression where the abuser exposes what is later to become commonplace in the relationship. The victim will not believe the outburst that she has just witnessed. She will look the other way or will make excuses. The excuses range from, 'he's tired', 'he's not feeling well' or 'it was my fault.'

UNREASONABLE EXPECTATIONS

Jade, 38
What mood will he be in when he comes through the door? I hope he hasn't been drinking – he'll be much worse then. I'm too scared to leave, but I'm also scared to stay. I'm chewing too loudly, speaking too loudly, being annoying and his most hated thing – not having the evening meal on the table at exactly the same time every night. His mother could do it, so why can't I get it right?

In Jade's example above, her partner has the unrealistic expectation that the dinner should be served at exactly the same time every day. If for some reason dinner wasn't on the table at the designated time, Jade would suffer for it and would be made to feel worthless. Her husband put unreasonable expectations on her, but he could not see this as he stated that his mother was able to have dinner on the table at the same time every night so why couldn't she? Picking on small things that don't really matter and blowing them into a major issue is a typical pattern of abusive behavior.

UNPREDICTABLE TEMPER

Anne-Maria, 53
I thought to be emotionally abused you would have to be meek and mild like a little mouse. I'm an emotionally stable intelligent woman who runs an extremely successful business and my husband is abusing me. The other night he started screaming and throwing things at me saying he hated me and wanted me to leave. I ran out of the house. I came back half an hour later and he was sitting watching television as if nothing had happened. I feel I am going mad.

Once the abuser has gotten away with their first display of temper and have suffered no consequences for their behavior, you can be sure that there is more of the same to follow. Until then the abuser snaps back to his lovely self and all is forgotten. The thing about emotional abuse is that it is intermittent and inconsistent. Once the abuse starts to become a common occurrence you will find yourself looking for signs of things that trigger it in an effort to avert an inevitable crisis. The victim will look to herself and think of ways she can modify some aspect of her behavior. Very often she will keep quiet and not say anything and if she does say something, it will be very carefully worded to avoid another outburst.

Very little things will often be the trigger the outburst and sometimes it appears that these triggers can be solely in the abuser's own mind. The victim will feel that she is walking on egg shells as she treads carefully to avoid triggering his temper.

When they're not abusing you, they can work very hard at being the man you've always wanted and you can think they are the love of your life. As an example, John would take great lengths to encourage me in my sculpture work and most days he would give me breakfast in bed. On the flip side though, if I happened to say what he considered to be 'the wrong thing' he would go 'cold' and a 'brick wall' would suddenly come up between us. He would go a whole day without saying a word. Very often the silent treatment and withdrawal of affection would continue into the next day. (Unfortunately on those days I *wouldn't* get breakfast in bed). Being with John was so tumultuous it was like being in a game of Russian roulette.

THE SILENT TREATMENT

Carla, 22
He showered me with attention and gifts and wanted to get married pretty quickly. Of course I agreed and things were good for a time. I'm

twenty-two and was abused as a child so I know what abuse feels like. This was the first abusive relationship I had been in since I left home. I don't even know where to start. One example is: I phoned him when he was at work and he didn't return my call. When he got home I found out he's mad at me about some little thing, which was really nothing. He made a big deal out of the smallest things and either he'd yell at me or wouldn't speak to me for days. I feel worthless.

What is the silent treatment? I've never quite understood the concept of the silent treatment; it's quite foreign to me. John is the only man and the only person who has ever delivered me the silent treatment. I guess it's designed to punish a person. The person who you are silent to is obviously in 'the wrong.' They may need this 'silent treatment' to figure out what they have done wrong and perhaps never do it again.

Or is this punishment meant to make the other person feel they are not worthy to be spoken to by the person giving the silent treatment? The only flaw in this type of behavior is that maybe the person giving the silent treatment should tell the person receiving the silent treatment what they have done wrong.

I believe every time I have had the 'silent treatment' I never knew what triggered it. I just went along with it and did my own thing. Well - what else was I to do? He obviously wasn't interested in having a conversation about it.

I can say that it hurt me, though. It hurt me that he didn't want to talk about things. It also showed a lack of respect for me. I like to talk things over – I'm not a fighter and I don't see the need for it in a relationship. There are always going to be disagreements in a relationship, but there is always some compromise, or at least you can agree to disagree – so why argue to the point of nastiness, name calling and yelling? It's degrading.

TECHNICAL DEFINITION OF EMOTIONAL ABUSE

It is only in the last ten years or so that emotional abuse has been defined and separated from other kinds of abuse. Prior to that, all abuse which was not physical was termed psychological abuse.

According to Health Canada emotional abuse is "based on power and control," and defines rejecting, degrading, terrorizing, isolating, corrupting/exploiting and "denying emotional responsiveness" as characteristic of emotional abuse.

* * *

Due to the controlling nature of an emotionally abusive relationship, other forms of abuse are sometimes entered into - such as verbal, financial or any of the other forms, but this is not always the case.

FIVE KINDS OF ABUSE

The following are five kinds of abuse identified by psychologists.

Physical

Physical abuse is not only hitting. It can also include: grabbing, pushing, pulling or shaking. Physical abuse is anything that hurts someone physically.

Verbal

Verbal abuse is name-calling, shouting, demeaning someone or putting them down.

Financial

Financial abuse isn't heard about very often. Sometimes the abuser will coerce the victim into giving them control over their finances. In other cases the spending of the victim will be at the discretion of the abuser, as the victim has to account for every cent. The victim is pressured into giving the abuser all their sign in authorization over all their accounts.

Sexual

Sexual abuse is when one partner is forced or coerced into having sex when they don't want it.

Emotional

Emotional abuse is subtler than the other forms of abuse. It can include sulking, withholding approval, attention or affection. Very often one partner controls the others important decisions most often regarding money. It can also involve controlling the way they dress or wear their hair.

***

No one can know or understand what it is like to be in an emotionally abusive relationship until they have lived through one. There are no physical scars on your body so others just don't understand. Emotional abuse can crush you and leave scars on your heart, as well as wound your spirit and your soul, and change you as a person.

WHY DO I FEEL A BOND WITH HIM AND WANT TO GO BACK?

In emotionally abusive relationships - as in other types of abusive relationships - once the victim leaves they often feel compelled to return to their abuser, myself included. I left and went back to my abuser so many times that I lost count. Why are these men so hard to leave? In Chapter 7 I explore a psychological phenomenon that takes place in the victim, causing so many to return the person who has abused them.

* * *

Victims of emotional abuse have forgotten what it is like to even have an opinion about something, let alone feel free to express that opinion. How do they even begin to contemplate putting their life back together when they don't even remember the person they used to be?

As painful as the relationship was it can't be forgotten or ignored. It would be nice to block it out or just ignore it, but you can't!

If you desire a normal romantic relationship at some point, or even if you just want to feel normal again, you must examine *how* and *why* you got into the abusive relationship, and *why* you let the abuse continue.

Why didn't you walk away when the abuse started?

These are key things to know before you can begin to move on and will be discussed in later chapters.

Chapter 2. DING DONG, WARNING SIGNS

Who are these people involved in emotionally abusive relationships? Who are the men who would abuse these women and who are the women who would put up with such treatment? The plain truth of it is that it could very well be you and probably is since you are reading this book.

The abuser is very clever and unpredictable. They can be lovely one minute and then next minute you can be left feeling crushed under their criticism and contempt, sometimes without them even saying a word.

If three or more of the following have occurred within your relationship on a consistent basis there is a good chance that you were or are in an abusive relationship.

THE ABUSER:

Controls you, with just a look of disapproval. The victim usually knows what ticks the abuse off and doesn't want that to happen, so the abuser has taught the victim his look of disapproval. If she complies with this and 'backs down' or changes what she was doing then the abuse is averted. Phew! Crisis averted!

Controls the finances. As abuse is about control it's very likely that the abuser also controls the finances, as that's a major part of peoples' lives. The victim often cannot get away from her abusive partner as he holds the 'purse strings.'

Constantly criticizes you. This is a staple for the abuser. He thrives on criticism - You are not good enough the way you are, and of course you do everything wrong! He wants to bring you down and in doing so build him a little perch, which is way above you.

Is rude to your friends and family. He is rude to your friends and family because he simply doesn't like them. Why? Because *you* do. Another reason? Because they are supporting you and they love you. He wants to be your sole support he wants *you* to *only* love him, he wants to have *all* of your attention. He also wants to kick out all support out from under you - by doing this he feels that he gets a tighter grip of control over you. Of course he doesn't like any of your friends and family!

Tries to isolate you. He may try to isolate you physically by not having access to a car or living in a remote area or he may try to isolate you by causing you to lose friends and lose communication with your family.

Tries to drive a wedge between you and the people you care about (which shuts off your support system). The reasons here are the same reasons he doesn't want you to talk to friends and family. He doesn't want you to have a support system. If you had a good support system you would tell them how he treats you and they would tell you to leave him. So if you don't have a support system you are left with only him in your life and that's what he ultimately wants.

May physically isolate you. He may physically isolate you by living in a remote place or refusing to let you go out without him. Both of these are done in an effort to make you totally dependent upon him.

May embarrass or belittle you in front of other people. Often they don't belittle you in public and only do it in private. However, some abusers do try to make you feel uncomfortable or embarrassed in public. This is done in an effort to make you feel small and worthless.

Shows little or no respect for you. In the start of the relationship you will get respect, but as the relationship continues this respect drops off. No one would yell at or demean someone they respect. Don't be under the delusion that your abuser respects you.

Doesn't talk things over with you as an equal partner. Simply and plainly you are not an equal partner. The abuser holds the power in this parent-child type of relationship. You may be more intelligent, you may know more about the subjects at hand than your partner does, but that doesn't matter - what he says goes. His decision is final and no discussion will be entered into.

Belittles your achievements. So you've got degrees or even a doctorate? *What does that mean, that's not impressive; anyone can get one of those. What are you doing with it anyway? You wasted your time with all that study.* You won a prize? *Anyone can win, just depends on how the judges are feeling on the day.* These are the typical 'put down' comments you have come to expect from your abuser in an effort to keep you 'below' them. Remember, they want to be the one sitting up on the perch.

Wants to know where you are all the time. They want to keep tabs on you because they want control not only over you, but also over what you are doing.

Insults you. The abuser is insulting you because he is insecure about himself. They insult you in an effort to feel better about themselves. This is often an outlet for their anger. They may also be doing it to start an argument so the other person will feel bad.

Humiliates you. The abuser sees that everything is your fault and never their own. A person who humiliates others is in turmoil themselves and doesn't know how to deal with what they are feeling. They lash out with insults and humiliate you because they often know of no other way to deal with you**.**

Want you to change your hair, your clothes or your general 'look.' Yes, you need to change because you aren't good enough how you are, are you? If you were good enough you wouldn't have to change. Some men make their women wear 'cover up' clothes so they don't need to be jealous because no man will look at you and some men want their women to look sexier to feed their ego. Whatever the reason it is controlling. They can have an opinion and 'likes' about what you wear, but warning bells should go off if they totally want to change your look so you feel and look like a different person.

Gives you the silent treatment. My favorite, the silent treatment. This is a form of punishment, which is designed to control you. He thinks it will also make you feel low and make you feel that you aren't good enough to be spoken to by him. You have obviously transgressed in a big way – You remember what you did, but often times you may not even know.

Has unpredictable moods. This is classic abusive behavior as it is designed to catch you off guard. If you knew what triggered the moods or when he would be angry that would make it too easy for you to deal with and to cope with. Unpredictability is the abuser's trump card, which he uses for full effect.

Withdraws affection. Abusers use this treatment much like the silent treatment; they 'shut down.' Their words are only grunts or monosyllables. Abusers think in treating you this way that you will see that you have displeased them and you deserve to be punished.

Wants your bank account details or PIN. What reason does he give for wanting your bank details? If you decide you want to share money or share a portion of your money then it's very easy to open a separate joint account for things you need to share such as groceries or the electric bill. Other than that it's not a good idea to hand over control of your money. What if you need to leave?

Wants your email and social media passwords. This is usually the sign of a jealous partner. He wants to check that you aren't speaking to any other love interest over the internet. You deserve your right to privacy. He has no right to demand to see what you have written to other people. This is an invasion of your privacy, even if you have nothing to hide; handing over you passwords is not good. Everyone is entitled to their privacy.

Reads your emails or goes through your phone. The type of person who wants your passwords will definitely go through your cell if you leave it lying around. Most people have social media and emails going to their phone so this is an ideal way for the abuser to find out who you are talking to and what you are saying. Very often they are scared you are thinking about leaving and they fear that you are speaking with other men.

Treats you like a child. You feel like a child in this relationship because that is how you are treated. He is the parent and you are the child. You ask permission and he says 'Yea or Nay'. If he says yes, then he is 'letting you' do something. Discussions rarely come into these relationships, dictating yes, discussions – rarely.

Will threaten to leave you. He wants attention and control. The end result is that you will turn yourself inside out, upside down or dance a jig to keep him happy.

Calls you stupid, dumb or ugly. He does this because he doesn't want you to leave. If you feel really bad about yourself you'll think that you can't get anyone else and you'll stay with him. Bottom line of this one is that the abuser is insecure. He doesn't really think that you are all these things. In fact, he thinks the opposite - that is what spurs him to say these horrid things to you.

Ignores your feelings or requests. Plain and simple - he is the boss and what he says goes. He controls this relationship and what you want or feel is of little concern to him.

Says you are too sensitive. Yes, this is a common thing that abusers say. If you get upset at all the horrible things he says or does it becomes your fault, not his. There's nothing wrong with him so it must be *you.* You're too sensitive.

Makes you feel there is something wrong with *you.* They make you feel like there is something wrong with you so you won't stop and think that it's them who has the problem. You are no match for him; manipulation has become an art form for him.

Has a rage of temper where he breaks things. Anger and temper drive these men. He may break things you love or he may punch holes in walls. He can't control his temper and needs an outlet.

Manipulates you by lying. Some abusers think nothing about lying to you. Since they have little respect for you, lying comes easily to them. I caught my ex John out on many lies over things that were so small it seemed lying wasn't even necessary. I think it just become a game to him, like making up a story for his own entertainment.

Says cruel things then says it was a 'joke.' This is their way of 'getting away with' saying very cruel things to you. You find it difficult to tell him you don't think it was funny because then you will be the one who "doesn't have a sense of humor". Who wants to be accused of not having a sense of humor? So again – we are back to you being the one with the problem, not him.

Makes unreasonable demands of you. The abuser will make unreasonable demands of you and want you to be perfect and do everything perfectly. Their goal is perfection and no one can live up to their ideals because they are totally unrealistic. The end result is that you feel that you don't measure up and are in some way lacking.

Is jealous and suspicious. These men by nature are often insecure and they fear you leaving them. They are often jealous and suspicious, which is why they need to know where you are all the time and who you are speaking to. They will go through your bag or your wallet and try to gain access to your phone or computer in an effort to 'check' up on you.

Continually questions your motives. A lot of these men are insecure and are not sure if you really love them. They question your motives about things so they can weigh up their next move in their mission to control you and your environment.

Things escalate when alcohol or drugs are involved. Things intensify when these mood-altering substances are involved. In my situation John had a severe problem with alcohol and would drink most nights and get much worse.

Needs you to ask his permission for everything. You need to ask permission because he is the person in charge. It's that simple. You no longer have free will if you are still in one of these relationships.

THE VICTIM:

You feel like you are 'walking on eggshells.' You never know what mood he'll be in and besides that you never know what you have said or done to trigger his temper. You can say something one day with no ramifications and when you say it the next day all hell will break loose. There is simply no consistency.

You are treated like a child. He treats you like a child because he has assumed the position as the person in charge. Often, you are treated as being not as clever as he and that is why he has to treat you like a child.

All decisions have to be cleared by the abuser. Just as a parent or a boss makes all the decisions, so too does the abuser make all the major decisions in these types of relationships. Often major life changing decisions will be made without him even consulting with you.

You constantly second guess yourself. You start to wonder if it's you who has the problem.

You just want his approval. You want his respect and his approval and no matter how hard you try – it just doesn't happen.

You have lost confidence in yourself. All your power has been handed over to your abuser. You forget who you used to be. If you've constantly been criticized and demeaned and even ridiculed of course you will lose confidence.

Your self-esteem has plummeted since the start of the relationship. Even if you began this relationship with a high amount of self-esteem it is normal that it plummets as you continual leave yourself open to this abuse.

You feel like there is something wrong with you. There is nothing wrong with you - your abuser wants you to think there is, so you won't realize that there is something seriously wrong with him. The only thing wrong that you did is that you didn't enforce your boundaries and tell him that you won't tolerate that behavior the first time it reared its ugly head. In a later chapter, setting and enforcing personal boundaries is discussed.

You are not talking to certain friends or family members due to his insistence. Abusers generally want you all to themselves. You are easier to control if you don't have a support system. When you are out of this relationship the best thing you can do is re-connect with people you have lost touch with. Even tell them what was happening to you, it's embarrassing sometimes to admit but you'll feel better once a few people know what you've been through.

You feel unlovable. You have been made to feel worthless, and all confidence has been stripped away. You are lovable. The first thing to do is learn to love yourself then you can allow others to come into your life who truly love and respect you.

You are scared of their temper. Their temper is violent and unpredictable. It's often the unpredictability that makes their temper so scary.

You feel like you don't "measure up." They have constantly criticized you, shamed you and put you down in an effort to make you feel worthless.

You try to keep the abuser happy at the expense of your own wants or desires. At the start of the relationship you want to keep them happy because you love them and want the best for them. Very often as the relationship progresses you may still love them, but it's now out of fear of them or their temper that you aim to keep them happy.

You feel unhappy and depressed. You know deep down you did nothing to deserve his treatment of you. In my relationship with John I couldn't understand how he treated me or why he thought so lowly of me that he could treat me the way he did.

You feel trapped with no way out. There are a myriad of reasons women can be trapped in relationships. There may be other people who would suffer in a divorce, such as children. You may be reluctant to leave considering the amount of effort and time that has been invested. There may be religious reasons to stay together. Chapter 6 goes into detail on different reasons why people feel compelled into staying in an abusive relationship. It's very easy for outsiders to think that abused people should get out of the relationship, but often there are many reasons that go towards it not being a straightforward decision.

You can't do anything right. You feel like you can't do anything correctly in these relationships, as everything you do is fair game for criticism. If you do things in one way you will be told that you should have done them another way. Nothing you do will be right.

You feel confused with nowhere to turn. You feel you are mad and you wonder if you really are. Is it me or is it him? Who do you tell? Very often you would have lost touch with people who were once close to you and your abuser is the only person you've been relying on. You feel alone and helpless.

You think twice before giving your opinion or don't give it at all. In these relationships you are very brave if you give your opinion - that is, if your opinion is in opposition to your abuser. It's often safer not to voice your opinion, but in doing so you are losing more of your sense of self.

You don't feel free to talk on the phone while he is there. Because the abuser likes to micromanage your life, he'll want to know who rang you, who texted you, what they said and what you said. The answers you give will leave you open to a lot of criticism. If you talk in front of him on the phone he will criticize what he can hear you saying. John used to do that when I was on the phone to my family. He said he couldn't believe that we didn't talk about current events or what is happening around the world. In the end I used to turn my cell phone off when he came home so I wouldn't have to speak to people in front of him.

Chapter 3. My Personal Story of Abuse

Like many people, I was caught up with the whole true love happily ever after 'Cinderella' type story, along with all the expectations. Boy meets girl and they live happily ever after.

I never bothered to read the fine print at the end, which says that some Prince Charmings really are toads in disguise whose sole purpose is to ruin every aspect of your life. (Okay, I'm exaggerating just a little, but I was blindsided by what happened to me).

So, once I had found my perfect man naturally I wanted us both to be happy and have a perfect life. I was in love with this man. He was quite a bit older; he was intelligent, successful and had a great sense of humor. I respected him as a person and respected his opinions.

Our relationship started fifteen years ago. I fell in love with him on the first date. He had something about him. He was witty, charismatic and charming.

John wasn't stereotypically handsome, but he made up for it in personality and to me he was everything I wanted.

We lived about twelve hours drive from each other. For the first twelve years we had an "on / off" long distance relationship. Not a good start, I know. It was always an intense roller coaster relationship with intense highs and just as intense lows. We never saw eye to eye, but somehow we were both always drawn back to each other.

At the eleven-year point we hadn't spoken for nearly a year due to a big argument. During that time we both seemed to change. Things seemed different when we finally started talking.

Being the modern forthright woman that I am, I informed him that I was in the market for a life partner and didn't want to keep going with the relationship if he wasn't interested in the same. He said that he was also looking for something permanent and long-term. This was the start of our last three years we shared together. I moved to where he lived so the long distance wouldn't be a problem, leaving behind my lucrative job.

My plan was that we would just "date" once I was in his city and see how things went. He suggested I take a larger apartment than I had originally intended and said that he would pay half of the rent. That way, he explained, it was close to his business and he would stay there a couple of times a week, as his house was further out of town.

Of course it sounded good to live in a nicer place, so I agreed. *I didn't know it at the time, but looking back this was my first mistake. I gave up my independence because in the end he didn't stay there a couple of times a week - he slept there EVERY night.* I didn't say anything – what could I say? This was the man I was in love with – surely I was happy he was there every night, right? The thing was if he had said, "Hey, let's move in together," I would have had to think about it further, but now – hey presto, we're living together.

I found a job in the city not far from where my (our) apartment was. I had to take a huge reduction in salary and after a few months I was struggling to keep up the mortgages on the two properties I owned. On top of this disaster, the global financial crisis hit which forced the value of my properties to plummet, so I couldn't even sell them to cover the mortgages. I ended up, on John's suggestion, having to go into voluntary bankruptcy. Could John have helped me financially? I hear you ask. Yes he could have, he was very wealthy. But he just stood by and let me go bankrupt (this isn't abuse per se, but now he controlled the finances).

In my new job I just couldn't settle in. The area was different, I was out of my comfort zone and pressure was put upon me by John to be home at a certain hour to cook dinner. After dinner, John would consume a lot of alcohol and get melancholy and start picking on me. *I was upset by this but figured it was just the alcohol talking.*

After a few months John persuaded me to leave where I was working and work in his business. I wasn't happy in my current job so I agreed to work for him. By then John had caused me to change my hair, change my clothes and change the jewelry I wore. He also criticized me any time I wanted to spend money even if it was just for a cup of coffee. **DING, DONG MAJOR WARNING BELLS!** – This is super controlling behavior!

He was upset when I talked to my family on the phone at night, saying it was 'not normal' to speak to them so much. (Ten minutes every few days is by no means excessive). *Ding, Dong! – driving a wedge between you and family! Controlling people like to cut off your support system, such as your friends and family.*

The first huge abusive moment (as if all of the above wasn't enough) happened when John said, "We've been here for months and there is that same piece of fluff near the front door. Why haven't you cleaned it?" I replied I hadn't noticed it and said that if he had noticed it then he should have picked it up, if it bothered him. In a temper, he threw the heavy vacuum cleaner he was holding with full force at my feet, it bounced up and hit me in the knee leaving a huge bruise. **WARNING BELLS,**

WARNING BELLS!! *What? What? I can't hear anything. Derrrr.*

At that point I felt a little trapped. I was living with this man, working for him, and had given up my independence and my previous life. I felt confident that things would work out because I 'loved' him and these are just little teething problems that all couples go through when they start living together, right? *Wrong. Yes, but isn't there an adjustment period for couples? Yes, people can ague and disagree, but when someone is continually criticizing and controlling their partner to the point of distraction, that is abusive.*

I had moved two states to be with him, so I had no friends in the whole state - I was eager to meet some people. I met a few people who I really liked and John was deliberately rude to them. We went out to dinner with a couple that I had recently met. I thought John would get along well with them. John started drinking heavily as soon as he sat down and then started belittling them. I felt super embarrassed, although they handled him fairly well.

He virtually told my friend she was stupid for being catholic and sending her children to a catholic school. It was extremely unacceptable and I felt really embarrassed. **WARNING BELLS, Ding Dong!** – controlling partners don't like you having friends.

I made the excuse for him that it was just the alcohol. (He promised to try to cut down on his drinking, which he did until I did something to 'annoy' him and then he would hit the bottle - hard).

Afterward it was just easier to socialize with his friends, until he would start to embarrass me in front of them. Oh, rewind, I forgot the lecture before we would go out with his friends – "*you are too quiet, they think you don't like them, blah blah*". (translated to mean, you are not good enough how you are and you need to change). **DING, DONG.**

He was always the life of the party and always liked to be the center of attention. Many times when we were out with his friends he would say something out of the blue to embarrass me. For example - "Tamara's a witch."

I would look horrified and say, "What are you talking about?" Then he would go on and on about me being a witch (I'm not, but should have put a spell on him a long time ago). They would laugh and I would just feel really embarrassed. - *Abusers like to embarrass and belittle.* **Dingalingaling!**

I knew that things weren't 'right". The fact that I felt like I was "walking on eggshells" all the time and felt like I couldn't relax and just be myself, gave me an inkling that there was something wrong with the relationship that I was in. The criticism was constant. Sentences would often start with – "People like you….." or "You and your family……"

I was criticized for holding my fork incorrectly, (my table manners are impeccable) missing a spot when I vacuumed the carpet, big things and small things - anything, whether warranted or unwarranted. No matter what I did, the criticism was incessant.

Sometimes he would be nice, understanding and loving. Other times he would go into a frenzied rage if I said the wrong thing. The trouble was, I didn't have any way of knowing which mood he would be in and what the 'wrong thing' to say would be.

I was constantly criticized, and so were my family and friends. I was demeaned and I was told I was stupid. I had spent many years studying and had gained many qualifications. However, he belittled all my achievements and called them 'useless' and told me I had 'wasted my time' getting my degrees.

He continually worked at driving a wedge between my family and myself as he had previously done with my friends.

I needed his approval for everything. He even controlled the clothing I bought and wore. If I bought cheap clothing, it was bad quality. If I bought good quality clothing it was too expensive and I was wasteful for spending so much money on myself. So I guess he wanted me to wear good quality designer clothing as long as it cost the same amount as the cheap clothing. I just couldn't win.

One year we were going to a formal function and he had 'approved' of what I planned to wear. At the last minute I changed what I was wearing because the weather was much hotter than expected. When he saw what I was wearing he said nothing, but when the day was over he got up close into my face and said, "Don't you ever do that to me again." I could hardly believe what I was hearing and needed him to clarify it (brave of me, I know). Apparently what I was wearing was not up to his 'standards' because it wasn't 'designer,' and he took it as a personal attack.

Leave, I hear you say? Yes, just LEAVE! In that three years we were together we had broken up and got back together so many times I cannot even count them. I craved his approval. I craved his acknowledgement of me. I felt 'at home' and comfortable when I was with him. He would blame his health issues and the stress of his business. He would promise to cut down on his drinking.

He wasn't like this all the time. Most of the time he was lovely and he had a soft side. That's what kept me there. The outbursts would catch me off guard and leave me confused and it was always much worse when he had been drinking.

I made excuses for his behavior, such as; 'he's improved,' 'he isn't well', and the fact that he had previously been in a very toxic relationship.

The beginning of the end of our relationship:

I thought about my future and the fact that I was in my early fifties, I had to have some sort of financial security for the future. I could see him building *his* financial future but not *our* financial future. I had gone bankrupt and had nothing so I knew I had to protect myself and have some sort of financial security. In my heart I knew I couldn't rely on him.

It's not that easy to just leave. In fact it was the hardest most heart-wrenching thing I have ever done in my life and it took a lot of strength. We had moved into a beautiful home and a good percentage of the time I was happy (although I always felt on guard as though I could never totally relax). In the end however, I did leave. I left with no money, nothing out of the house, no job, not even my personal possessions. I left with just some of my clothes. (He had agreed to send the rest of my things, but I'm still waiting). It wasn't just leaving him; it was leaving my whole environment, my whole world. It was hard, but I just knew I had to do it.

I expected to feel better straight away. I had left the abuse, so why didn't I feel better? I felt worthless. I felt not good enough. If I *was* 'good enough' then he wouldn't have treated me the way he had. Would he? Why didn't *he* think I was good enough to treat me better, what's wrong with me?

At first I went through grieving and the pain of loss and then loneliness. Then came the extreme anger. I felt that he had ruined me and ruined my life. I was once a vitally independent person who was once financially well off and because of the circumstances surrounding my moving to be with him, I had lost all my money along with my confidence and self-esteem. I felt broken and crushed; I literally had not a penny to my name, which made me feel like a speck of dirt.

I went into a deep state of depression. Thinking things such as – 'Most people my age own their own home' and 'most people my age are thinking about retirement.' If things weren't bad enough through lack of money I was forced to live with relatives.

When I was recovering I had to admit that I had a pattern of abuse prior to this abusive situation made me realize I had to 'reprogram my mind and my thoughts.' I was truly a mess and recovery was by no means instant. I had to rebuild, not only my outer world, but also the inner world in my head.

I knew John had a huge problem and I knew how he had acted toward me, yet I felt drawn back. It didn't make sense.

The things that helped me through my difficult times were learning what abuse is and why I put up with it for as long as I did. Learning the reasons why I was drawn back also helped me to recover.

I wouldn't be where I am today without positive thoughts, visualization and meditation which all worked together to reprogram my mind.

My path back to normality wasn't easy, but there was only one way to go – one step at a time.

I share all that I found to be helpful in the following chapters.

Chapter 4. Victim's Stories of Emotional Abuse

It helped me to know I wasn't alone and that there were other women and men, out there who were going through, and had been through, relationships that were emotionally abusive. Once I publicly shared my story, many people approached me to tell me what happened to them. With their permission, I reveal their experiences. (Names are changed to protect their privacy).

Sharon, 42
I found myself giving into his demands. I wore flat shoes and loose casual clothing which didn't reveal too much skin. I also kept my cell phone close so I could answer it quickly when he called. If I didn't do these things he would yell at me.

Jocelyn, 51
While he was overseas for work, I discovered a cigarette lighter advertising a brothel in one of his suit pockets. I rang him and questioned him about

it. He made some excuse, which sounded reasonable. Then he started shouting and swearing at me. All through that night I got several drunken phone calls with him abusing me. He made me feel bad for not trusting him.

Lisa, 34
I would never speak in front of him on when I was on my cell phone, because if he could hear what I was saying he would get nasty and criticize my conversation even when it was nothing to do with him.

Amanda, 26
I cut my hair short because that's the way he liked it even though it made me feel like I wasn't feminine. I stopped seeing my friends because he didn't like them. He would lose his temper over little things. He always had to know where I was and he even phoned the dentist when I was having my teeth fixed to check that I was really there.

Sandra, 23

My boyfriend left me for another girl. He was abusing me. I found out he is now abusing his new girlfriend and I am upset and jealous. I know it's weird but I miss him and want him back.

Bella, 24

It was really tough to leave. He had been the central person in my life for so long. I still feel I want to phone him every time something major happens in my life. I just want to tell him about it. I have to bring myself back to reality and see him for what he is. I knew there was nothing that could make him change because he wouldn't admit to having a problem. He always told me it was me who had the problem.

Kendra, 21

Six months after I left him he phoned me to ask how I was. Then he told me that I never finish anything I start. He was pushing my buttons again. I should've just hung up. I spoke of all the things I'd finished and asked what he was speaking of to make such a statement. He changed the subject. A few minutes later he said it again. This time I just hung up. He wants to make me angry then it makes me look like I'm the crazy one.

Jackie, 51
I look back and remember his sister calling him Jekyll and Hyde. I also remember he would control his mother by either sulking or losing his temper. We were both scared of his temper. I guess he had the pattern going way before I came along. I got depressed and gained nearly forty pounds. When I left, my weight gradually went back to normal.

Sally, 34
My partner was dishonest and secretive. I never knew things like how much money we had. He just would shut down when I tried to find out. He didn't want to listen to my opinion about anything and the way he talked to me made me feel like I was stupid. I always felt that somehow I was on a lower level

than him and that we weren't equal. I tried many times to tell him how he was making me feel, but it just made him angry and then he wouldn't talk to me for days.

Celia, 29

Even though he has never done any housework he says I'm not doing it right. He is never satisfied with anything I do; even the pantry is never arranged correctly. It's gotten to the point that whatever I do I know he's going to correct it. Once he got so angry that I hadn't set the table correctly that he picked up a large plate and smashed it on the floor. He's rude to me in public, which is hugely embarrassing to me. I never wanted to be one of those couples that argue in public. He snaps at me or puts me down. He used to be so nice, now he's cranky and upset all the time, usually it's something I did or didn't do properly. When I get upset he either says I'm too sensitive or tries to make out he was joking. He's continually angry with me for no reason. I'm concerned that I walk on eggshells around him so I don't upset him. We can have a good day as long as it's on his terms. I can never consider leaving because we have two small children.

Jessica, 27
He had a severe drinking problem. Everything got much worse when he was drinking. I just used to stay out of his way as much as I could. He would say hateful things to me out of the blue. It was like he didn't live in the same world as me. He would make things up to accuse me of.

Kandi, 28
Nothing I did was ever right and he constantly picked on me. I didn't dress right, I didn't speak right, I shouldn't have done this shouldn't have done that. Why didn't I do it this way, why didn't I do it that way? In the end I stopped trying to please him because nothing made any difference.

Lynne, 49

He started off being just emotionally and verbally abusive. Then one time in an argument he grabbed my wrist very hard and pulled me across the room. I had huge bruises for days. He didn't care and didn't even acknowledge it when I showed him the bruises. One time when we were arguing he put his hands around my throat. I yelled at him, "Go on kill me." At that point I didn't even care if I lived or died. He let go of my throat.

Margaret, 38

He was so horrible to me I would sit in the bathroom and cry like a baby. I'm a professional person and everyone I work with treats me with a lot of respect. Why can't I get this respect from the man I love? When I'm at home he makes me feel wretched and I feel like I can never do anything to make him happy with me. Once I spent hours cooking his favorite meal, then he got angry with me for some tiny reason and then he wouldn't eat it. He would drive me to frustration and anger. Then he said that my temper was the reason for our problems.

Todd, 27
He always told me if I left I wouldn't be able to get anyone as good as him. He made me believe that no one else would want me. He almost had me thinking that there was something seriously wrong with me. His temper was uncontrollable. I wondered if I didn't deserve a better life. Don't get me wrong, there were good times. Now I feel like a fool for staying in the relationship for so long.

Jane, 42
My husband and best friend left me six months ago for another woman. He was everything to me. We have two children together. Even though we aren't together he still tries to control and manipulate me. He tells me I'm a bad person and a bad mother. But, I know I'm not. I don't know why he says those things. I was very young when we got married.

Chelsea, 19

Things were super to begin with, but that changed about a year into our dating. He would sulk and be cranky at me just for saying hello to a boy I knew who was walking past us. He was jealous if he thought I was even looking in the direction of another boy. He always accused me of flirting. Then he started getting angry about lots of other things. I wasn't allowed to have friends he didn't know. He decided we could only have mutual friends.

Nigel, 53

I am a middle-aged man and have been abused by my wife. None of my friends can understand what I have been through except one of them. I cry every night. She took over control of everything, constantly screamed at me and made me feel stupid and worthless. I've left her and now and as a consequence I have very little money. I wonder what's wrong with me for this to have happened.

Stephen, 26

She always told me it was me who had the problem. She said my family was dysfunctional and so was I, that's why I didn't know what was right and what was wrong. She really f.... with my head. I went back to her once after I left, it only lasted six months then I left for good. I'm too scared to have another relationship for fear of it turning out the same.

David, 35
She left me and I should be happy without the abuse. I don't know how to be happy. I just feel numb. I fear by entering another relationship I'd be dumping all this sh…. on another person. I have so many problems now. I just want to be happy again.

Ilsa, 39
I suffered abuse for many years. Then he shouted at me for three whole days to leave. He would say, 'you go or I'll go.' In the end I said that I would go. He was shocked. He cried and cried and said that he didn't mean it. My heart was shattered into a

million pieces. I was shouted at for three days to leave and that was a joke? To me, that was worse than if he had meant it. I left and never went back.

Tessa, 33
I told him how much he was upsetting me. He said that he wondered if he was somehow "testing" me to make sure I would always stay with him. I only realize now as I write this, that in saying that, he has turned the blame back toward me – I 'failed' the test in not being able to make it through all that abuse. Or was he sharing his feelings? That is what it's like being with an abuser; you never know what's real and what's not because they are artful liars and manipulators.

Wendy, 44
We were on a special holiday. At the end of the day I was sitting on the bed. He got very upset and said to me that it was 'his side.' I said, 'all right, I don't really care, you sleep on this side then.' Without saying a word he took a pillow and spent all night

on the couch. The next night we were watching television in the hotel bed. He was watching some sporting game (not the finals). I asked him if we could watch something we would both be interested in. Without saying a word, he turned off the television, turned off the lights and went to sleep.

Mandy, 52
My husband bought my 21-year-old son (from a previous marriage) a car. Then he wanted to control my son like he controls me. He wanted to know where he was all the time and what he was doing. He also wanted my son's log in details to his bank account. My son told him to mind his own business so my husband took the car away.

Chapter 5. Profile of the typical abuser

__Kevin:__ I never thought of myself as an abuser. I would never dream of hitting anyone. Knowing what I know now, I admit that I used emotional and verbal abuse on my wife, Julia. Julia left me two years ago after a year of begging me to go to counseling. I never liked the idea of talking to a therapist or the likes; I'd always seen that as the end of a relationship. I had a hard time adjusting to life after Julia divorced me and an even harder time when I heard she was engaged to another fellow nearly a year after that. I went to the doctor for some pills to make me feel better. He was very forceful in wanting me to go to a therapist. I agreed.

After two sessions I realized what I had put Julia through. I didn't like myself for what I had done. I had an overly critical father and I even remember saying things to Julia, word for word, things my father had said to me. Bottom line is that I always wondered what she saw in me and I think I was frightened she would leave me one day. I think

I was testing her, or hastening the inevitable. I've gone on a couple of dates, but I don't think I'm cured. As awful as it sounds, I find myself looking for clues to their vulnerability. It's almost as if they are an opponent in some sort of mind game.

* * *

Abusers have all come from the same cookie cutter. They may look different, come from different social backgrounds and have different jobs, but they've all read the same handbook. If you've read my story and stories of other victims you will see common threads running through each one of them. I've even read stories and they sound exactly the same as my own because the very same things happened to me.

I use the word abuser in this book, which is probably not a good idea, as it conjures up a picture of a villain, or a bad person. In reality, the abuser is sometimes charming and very complimentary towards you. They draw you in with their charm, wit and charisma. Very often they are the life of the party and everyone loves them. You will have no idea this lovely man is an abuser until you're committed to the relationship. By then they have noted your strengths and your weaknesses. They've found out which buttons to press so they can gain control. Sure there may have been warning signs along the way, but you conveniently ignored them, didn't you?

These abusers are typically described as being like Dr. Jekyll and Mr. Hyde, which are two opposite personalities in the one person. They can be delightful one minute then in a flash they are horrendously nasty. Typically this will take place in private. Their unpredictability is specifically designed to catch you off guard. When confronted about his behavior the abuser has the ability to twist events to make it look like he is the victim.

In the book the Mind of the Abuser, Dr Vaknin states the following. "The abuser makes sure that *HE* is the only reliable element in the lives of his nearest and dearest – by shattering the rest of their world through his seemingly insane behavior. He perpetuates his stable presence in their lives – by destabilizing their own."

Chloe 25, Brisbane
We had just moved into a new apartment. He yelled at me because the dishwasher was filthy and what a filthy person I was because I thought that the filthy dishwasher was acceptable. I replied that I hadn't looked at it, and that it wasn't my fault and I would phone the agent. In the end I just had to sit there and listen to what a filthy person I was to not notice the filth in the dishwasher. He insisted on cleaning it himself while I had to sit there, watching him heave in between berating me. Every now and again he would put the dirty cloth just inches away from my face so I could see the filth that was as 'filthy' as I was. I felt like I was a bad person and I should've noticed that the dishwasher was dirty before we moved in.

The abuser is a bully, but a lot of bullies have low self-esteem and out of fear, feel a need to control both their partner and their environment. They do what they need to do to have control, which includes lying, manipulating and even yelling and / or smashing things. They feel that as long as they aren't hitting or being physically violent, then that's okay.

The abuser may appear confident, but that only masks their inner tumultuous world. As well as having low confidence, low self-esteem they are often immature and almost always emotionally absent.

What caused them to be like this?

Is it biological or have they been socialized into this abusive behavior pattern? Are the men who abuse, confused by our patriarchal society which leads them into the false assumption that they have the right to dominate and control women?

Or is it nature? Do they have a biologically issue that triggers the abuse? Three personality disorders that have been identified which may contribute to abusive behavior.

BIOLOGICAL REASONS FOR ABUSE

The three disorders listed below have been categorized by the updated (2013) Diagnostic and Statistical Manual of Mental Disorders. (Known as the DSM V) as dramatic, emotional or erratic disorders.

*Narcissistic personality disorder.
People with this disorder have a sense of entitlement. They are vain and self-centered. They require the admiration of others, exaggerate their accomplishments, exploit others and are preoccupied with power and prestige. They are egocentric.

*Antisocial personality disorder.
People with this disorder show disregard for others, whether it is towards an individual or society as a whole. They lie; they are aggressive and have no remorse for their actions. They have a lack of

morals and exhibit compulsive and aggressive behavior.

*Borderline personality disorder.

People who have this disorder often have an intense fear of abandonment. They may exhibit intense anger and irritability. They often engage in the idealization and devaluation of others, alternating between high positive regard and great disappointment. These people can be suicidal or indulge in self-harm.

SOCIAL CAUSES

Our society has a long history of the subjugation of women. It wasn't all that long ago that women were seen as the property of men. We have only recently had the privilege of voting and equal pay is still not a reality. Men are brought up in an environment which nurtures the notion that men are the stronger sex and are somehow superior to women.

Does this make men feel they have to control their women? Does it make these insecure males feel like a 'man' when they are abusing?

The abuser has typically been abused as a child or may have been abused in a previous relationship. They are often severely sensitive people who have found a very negative outlet for their desire to feel safe. They feel safe when they have total control of their environment and the people around them. The overwhelming desire to control their spouse flows over into every aspect of their spouse's life. Some abusers have a deep-seated fear of abandonment.

YOU CAN'T HELP YOUR ABUSER

Resist any attempt to help your abuser. The help is best to come from professionals. Channel your efforts into helping yourself.

If you have ever tried to talk to your abuser you will notice that the abuser always justifies their behavior and often turns it around to make you think that *you* have the problem. They can't see that it is *they* who have the problem as they have the ability to justify and even twist events in their own minds.

Whatever the cause of the abuse, the abuser is deliberate, the abuser is calculating and the abuser is unfeeling to the victim. The abuse is designed to crush and control you.

Chapter 6. Profile of the typical Victim

One word describes these people – People pleasers! Oh wait, that's two words. Anyway, abused people are usually 'people pleasers' which means that they put their own needs last on a continual basis. If this describes you – it's okay to say 'no' sometimes.

Anyone can become the victim of abuse. However, people who are confident and feel good about themselves, on a deep inner level, will usually leave at the first or second sign of abuse. Whereas the women with an inner feeling of unworthiness or a feeling that they somehow don't measure up, will stay and make excuses for the first signs that all is not well.

You love this man so much that you want this romance/marriage to last forever. We so badly want our perfect life that we overlook all the little things that are said and done until it comes to the point when we suddenly realize we are living with a Jekyll and Hyde monster.

SOCIAL CAUSES

Western women have been taught to be good polite 'people pleasers'. It isn't surprising that women have the desire to please, often putting everyone else before themselves. We have been socialized in to being nice, giving, unselfish, accommodating, to be the peacemaker and the nurturer. We are given dolls to play with and taught to be a 'good mother.' We have been brought up to be the nurturer in all relationships at the expense of nurturing and looking after ourselves. It is these qualities that make it easy for the abuser to abuse. Add to that a dash of low self-esteem and a lack of a 'sense of self' and it's a recipe for disaster.

I'm not saying that women should become selfish cows. I'm saying women should treat themselves with the same respect that they show to other people. Women need to stop putting themselves last and start putting themselves first.

The women who end up being abused are the ones who have handed control of their life over to another often without realizing it.

Most western women have been brought up to believe the myth that Prince Charming is going to come along, look after them and solve all their problems. We look to the man to be the provider and the protector. The patriarchal society we live in sets men up to believe that they should be above the woman - the man is the dominating force and the woman is lesser. If you think bra burning and women's lib has fixed that, you're wrong. We have come a hell of a long way, but things like equal pay for all is still not a reality.

The fairy tales little girls are told actually end up working against them. Laugh at me if you will, but I blame all those fairy tales and movies that end up with the man swooping the woman off her feet, they have a whirlwind romance, and then they live happily ever after. These unrealistic romantic tales have caused little girls to spend years thinking about their wedding, their wedding dress, how many bridesmaids they'll have, who will walk them down the aisle – the list goes on. They have it all planned out before they even meet the man. They give so many years of thought to the wedding and hardly any thought goes into the relationship after the wedding, and whether this person has what it takes to sustain their interest for a further fifty years. More importantly the inner qualities that this man has is very often assumed rather than confirmed.

Life isn't like a fairy tale. I guess it can be, but to assume that the man you have just started to date is going to be 'your everything,' 'your provider,' is 'going to look after you,' is in my opinion, a dangerous thing.

Although women are strong and capable a lot of us think that we've nothing without a man. It's often hard for a single woman to socialize especially if all her friends are married. If she were married it's a comfortable idea that couples can go out to dinner together. Not so comfortable when a couple go out to dinner with a single friend. Most invitations to events are to a person and their guest, their 'plus one.' Life's just a heck of a lot more convenient and often a lot more fun if you have a significant other. It's not much fun going on a holiday by yourself and you can't put 'flat pack' furniture together by yourself either.

The sensitive, nurturing side of the woman is quick to give up their own wants, needs and goals in favor of their partners. The victim can start out believing that they are strong and independent, but slow and insidious changes take place as little behaviors or events are ignored and before they realize it they have handed all their power over to their partner.

* * *

Often the victim has been in other controlling situations in the past, whether it was in childhood with controlling parents or in a previous relationship. Often they were abused as a child by way of neglect, witnessing abuse or even by having over critical caregivers. In my own example, I was in a strictly controlled religious environment with extremely critical parents even before my first husband came along.

ABUSED PEOPLE HAVE THE FOLLOWING IN COMMON
They often:
*Put other people before themselves. Many women put others before themselves. That is what we've been taught to do as women. We are taught to nurture others; we weren't taught that we should nurture ourselves and look after ourselves. We were taught that a man would look after us and care for us. Women have a hard time spending money on themselves. I worked in retail for a while when I was in college and I noticed how women would feel guilty if they spent money on themselves. If this describes you, go out now and spend some money on yourself, buy some clothes or get your nails done – do something for yourself, and don't feel guilty about it!

*Lack self-esteem, and confidence; deep down they just don't feel good about themselves. If a woman felt good about herself she would put her foot down and not accept such behavior. The abuser would either have to comply or move on.

*Need validation of themselves, which they try to obtain from the abuser. The abused person often only feels good about themselves when they have the abusers permission to do so by way of their approval.

*Don't have boundaries. If they do, they don't follow through on them. In my experience I had boundaries, but once those boundaries were pushed I failed to enforce them. I just let myself be railroaded. I put all my trust in the abuser's hands.

*Try and keep their partner happy. We figure if the abuser is happy then everyone will be happy. It's very hard to keep an abusive partner happy though as they are very changeable in what will make them happy.

*Haven't learned from past experiences. Most people, once they have been in an abusive relationship, fall into other abusive relationships unless they deliberately stop the cycle.

*Let their partner walk all over them and do nothing. In Chapter 7 you will learn how to set boundaries and how to enforce those boundaries once they are pushed against. You need to be strong though.

*Make excuses for their partner's behavior. Saying things like, 'he has improved; he said he wouldn't do it again, it was my fault.

*Feel that they are somehow a bad person. When you've been some time in an abusive relationship you lose confidence and self-esteem and figure you must be a bad person for them to treat you the way they do.

*Are confused by their partner's behavior. The abuser is often unpredictable and unreasonable, so their behavior leaves you totally confused as you try to make sense of it.

*Don't tell anyone about the abuse. It's tempting not to tell anyone. It's embarrassing to admit to people that your relationship is so horrible particularly when people think you have a great relationship. Often the abuser keeps his best work away from the public eye.

Do nothing and hope it goes away. Sometimes it's hard for the person who is being abused to know what to do. They really don't want to admit it to themselves or other people so it's easier to do nothing and hope that somehow their relationship will become good.

* * *

Once someone experiences a toxic relationship why are they more likely to repeat the pattern?

It's simply true that people who have experienced an abusive relationship are more likely to end up in another one. The patterns that the victim has established need to be identified realized and unlearned before another relationship is entered in to. That is if they wish to break the pattern of abuse.

Until lessons are learned and mistakes are realized the pattern will just keep repeating. The smaller percentage who have a relationship with an abuser and then go on to have a healthy relationship are the same people who have learned what contributed to the pattern of abuse in their life.

How do you approach relationships? Chances are if you have been in an abusive relationship you will recognize some of these behaviors listed below.

*Do you get attached to a new person too quickly, before you really get to know them? In my experience with John I felt I loved him after one date. I couldn't have fallen in love with him so quickly because I didn't even know him. I didn't know if he had all the qualities I was looking for in a person and I didn't know if he had any bad or objectionable habits. I didn't know what his morals or beliefs were. So why did I feel that I was in love with him after one date? Damned if I know!

*Do you hope that he is your Prince Charming? Do you hope that he is 'the one'? Where did this come from I wonder, 'the one'? This hasn't been helpful in relationships. Most people want to find 'the one' instead of starting out friends then seeing what develops over time.

*Do you crave to have a permanent relationship? Do you long to find that one person rather than continually dating? Do you want to stop kissing all those frogs? While there's nothing wrong with that, there is something wrong with finding a person and trying to talk yourself into the fact that they are 'the one' - and then you try to make them fit all your ideals.

*Do you see slight signs of compulsion within yourself? I find that I am compulsive in a lot of ways. I must finish things that I start and I will work obsessively till it is finished. I am also extremely competitive and want to win at everything I'm involved in. I think in this way I became a little obsessive over John and held him in higher esteem than he observed, I was blinded by my compulsion to have a good relationship with him.

If you answered yes to any one of these questions you are already in the danger zone of getting into another bad relationship.

You may realize you need to change your dating thinking but don't know how. It's very likely that your abusive relationship was very quick and intense to begin with. See how to change your patterns in Chapter 11.

Chapter 7. Why don't you just leave?

Women are often stuck in these relationships with abusive men with nowhere else to go. There may be children involved or they may have no access to finances. Prevention is the best cure. Never let anyone else have total control over your finances, even if you don't work and your partner does, you need to negotiate that you have access to money. It is also important to retain your own friends and your own independence.

There are a myriad of reasons that keep people in relationships, even when the relationship has turned sour.

Time.

Time is a number one factor that people give for staying in a relationship. You've developed a long history together. Putting any feelings aside, in my own experience, I was reluctant to leave because of the time factor. I had fifteen years invested and I didn't want that to all come to nothing.

I can help him get better.

Some victims are under the mistaken impression that they can help the abuser change. The abuser may improve, but unless he is willing to change and unless he admits to having a problem he will only revert back to his old ways.

I feel sorry for him.

Being sorry for someone is a poor excuse for being in an abusive relationship. The abusers may have been abused themselves, but unless they are aware of their abusive behavior and wish to change there seems to be no point in staying in the relationship.

I committed to it.

A lot of people with very strong beliefs, such as religious beliefs, feel they must stay in a bad relationship, for better or worse.

He's not like it all the time.

Most abusers are not abusive all the time. When they are nice they are nice and when they are not, they are really horrible. Their inconsistency is deliberate in their attempt to gain control.

He doesn't hurt me physically.
There are other ways to hurt people than physically. Emotional and verbal abuse hurt your soul and your spirit and the scars left are often permanent.

All relationships need work.
That may be true but both parties have to be willing to make it work, and an abusive relationship needs a special kind of work - which you aren't able to give it. You can't even talk to him without making yourself a possible target for abuse.

The abuser is familiar.
As the saying goes, better the devil you know than the devil you don't know. For some there is comfort in what is familiar, and others fear change and all that goes along with it. You have gotten into a habit with him - and habits are hard to break.

Staying is easier than leaving

You have gotten to know what ticks him off. So you just figure you'll lay low and hopefully it will sort itself out one day. What will you do if you leave? In some ways it may be easier to stay. You have to weigh up the pros and cons and ask yourself what you want out of life. For me, the biggest thing I want out of life is peace and serenity, which I have now that John is out of my life.

Family

There may be children involved, which can make leaving difficult. However, if there are children involved it may be a very good reason to leave, if the partner refuses therapy. Research has shown that children thrive in a happy environment even if that means that their parents are no longer together. So never use the children as an excuse to stay, as they are better off away from conflict. Children are always watching and always learning. There is a danger that they will view the dysfunctional relationship as normal and repeat that with their own relationships. There may also be elderly parents or other family members who would suffer with the dissolution of the relationship.

Social Reasons

Some people are embarrassed that their social set will find out that their relationship is not perfect. Often abusive people only abuse their partner at home or in a safe environment, there are rarely witnesses to the abuse. Many people feel it would be an embarrassment if people found out the truth about the relationship, so the charade lives on at the victims expense. It is embarrassing to admit to anyone that you let him treat you that way.

You think you won't be able to get anyone else

Often the abuser has become the center of the victim's world. They don't want anyone else, nor can they even imagine being with anyone else. My ex partner used to tell me all the time that I would never be able to get anyone as good as him. This is the mission of the abuser, to lower the victim's self-esteem so it's easier for them to gain control and to have the victim think that they have nowhere else to go.

Finances

In a lot of relationship the abuser controls all the money giving little or no access to their partner making it very difficult for the victim to leave. Other people stay for the lifestyle they have with their partner fearing they will get little or no money if they leave.

Fear of being alone

Some figure someone is better than no one. It can be frightening out there in the big wide world especially if the victim has no friends or family for support. What these people don't realize is that being alone can be beneficial. There is no one to check up on you. You can do whatever you want to do. Eat what you want when you want, you can eat ice cream at midnight or crackers in bed. Go wherever you want and see whomever you want to see. You don't even have to compromise. When you are alone you get to have exactly what you want without having to check in with someone or make compromises.

They don't realize they are being abused
It's a sad fact that many people don't even realize they are being abused. In my first marriage, it was pointed out to me by other people, that my husband was being verbally abusive. I didn't even realize I was being abused I just thought that it was normal.

* * *

The longer a couple is together the more their lives become entwined and entangled. Friends and finances are often shared; so much that it makes leaving, even if there is abuse, very difficult.

It is much easier to leave at the beginning of the relationship as soon as you realize that you have an abuser on your hands.

Chapter 8. Why do so many victims return to their abuser?

A huge percentage of victims of emotional abuse are known to return to their abuser. Why? It doesn't really make sense does it? Why would an intelligent woman return to a man who has repeatedly abused her? Is it love? I heard somewhere that **love is a behavior, not a feeling**. That has stuck with me because it's very true.

He would tell me he loved me over and over, yet his treatment of me said something that was in opposition to the word 'love.' Although I knew this in my head my heart was feeling something different. I had strong feelings for him even a year and a half after I had left him. I missed him so much that every time I thought about him I was still very emotional and would be on the verge of tears, which I would fight back. I don't know if I would say that I loved him, as I felt betrayed and had lost respect for him, but I still felt such a strong connection as if he were part of me, part of my family. I felt like we belonged together. I felt so comfortable when I was with him. I still couldn't see myself with anyone else. My feelings mystified me.

I used to think there was some deep mystical reason why I felt a strong connection to John? Even to the point that I thought we may have been lovers in former lives – even though I'm not sure if there are former lives or not.

In my heart I felt that was the only one for me and I couldn't see myself with anyone else. Long after leaving I would daydream and imagine that he was there with me. I would sit in a café and imagine he was there next to me. I would remember what it felt like to have his arms around me. In my daydream he was always nice to me.

Even though I couldn't take his volatile nature anymore and vowed that I deserved peace and serenity in my life, I still found that I was torturing myself with my thoughts of whether or not I had done the best thing in leaving.

Although I was no longer in a relationship with the man who had abused me – why was I still obsessing over him and why couldn't I get him out of my head?

It's normal to have second thoughts and wonder if you did the right thing leaving when you did. You probably have thoughts going through your mind such as:

Should I have stayed and made him go to therapy?

Could I have helped him?

Many women leave and go back, but does anything ever really change? I had left and gone back so many times and nothing had ever changed. He had improved, he stopped lying about everything and I could see how he was making an effort, but he was still very abusive toward me.

My research led me to two theories, which explained why women a feel a strong love connection to the men who abuse them.

One is called the 'Stockholm Syndrome'; the other is called 'Trauma Bonding'. In both of these the victim forms an attachment to the abuser as the body's 'survival mechanism.'

Stockholm syndrome is named after a bank robbery in Stockholm, in which several bank employees were strapped with dynamite and held hostage in a bank vault from August 23 to August 28, 1973, while their captors negotiated with police. During their ordeal the victims became emotionally attached to their captors, rejected assistance from government officials at one point, and even defended their captors after they were freed from their six-day ordeal. Some of the hostages even paid for the legal fees of the bank robbers.

The psychological phenomenon, which the hostages exhibited, came to be known as the 'Stockholm syndrome'. The hostages' feelings didn't make sense as they were in danger of their lives so their feelings were totally irrational. However, this is not an isolated case as the FBI has recorded that in 27% of hostage cases the captives have shown evidence of the Stockholm syndrome.

Stockholm Syndrome produces an unhealthy bond with the controller and abuser. It is the reason many victims continue to support an abuser after the relationship is over. It's also the reason they continue to see "the good side" of an abusive individual and appear sympathetic to someone who has mentally and sometimes physically abused them.

Stockholm syndrome can be seen as a form of **traumatic bonding**, which describes the incredibly strong emotional ties that develop between two people where one person, on an intermittent basis harasses, beats, threatens, abuses, or intimidates the other person.

Trauma bonding is, psychologically speaking, a survival mechanism. Our primal instinct ensures that by the victim feeling love and a feeling of *connection* with your abuser, the victim can maintain survival, and ultimately aid in the survival of the species.

Realizing that I had something psychological, which was making me feel this bonding, really aided me to recover. It wasn't love, it wasn't romantic, and it wasn't even real. In fact, I only felt this love and this connection because my brain had shut down and was in survival mode.

Traumatic Bonding. The theory of traumatic bonding is where strong emotional attachments are formed between two people where one intermittently harasses, threatens, abuses, intimidates or beats the other. (Dutton & Painter, 1981). The following conditions occur for the traumatic bond to occur.

*There is an imbalance of power, where one sets themselves up as the 'authority' such as controlling finances, or making the important decisions often using subtle intimidation or threats. The relationship is not equal.

*The abuse is intermittent in nature. There are alternating highs and lows, such as intense kindness and then the negatives of the abusive behavior.

*The victim is in denial of the abuse for emotional self-protection. The victim may experience cognitive dissonance where they change their perception of reality because they cannot comprehend the truth of what is happening. The mind distorts reality allowing the victim to survive.

*The victim does not tell anyone that the abuse is happening, sometimes not even admitting it to themselves.

The victim finds it difficult to break away from the relationship because their traumatized mind is in a false state of reality, in survival mode, causing them to feel a bond to their abuser. Once however they realize why they are feeling the way they are, that there is a valid reason for them to feel this way it is a lot easier to cope with those feelings.

What he did to you has made you go into survival mode. This person was supposed to love you and protect you.

HOW TO DEAL WITH YOUR EX ONCE YOU HAVE LEFT

It is best to have no contact with your ex once you have left. It would be nice to be able to be friends, but if someone has abused you they aren't acting like a friend and don't deserve your time. I've found that the put downs continue whether you are in a relationship or not. Obviously, if you have children you will have to have contact with them but it is best to keep it to a minimum where possible.

Don't let them back into your life. These men have charmed their way into your life at least once so they know how to do it. They are master manipulators and liars and they know where all your buttons are so beware!

If you have to, block them on social media and block their phone calls. If you keep contact with them don't think that the put downs and insults will stop, because they won't. Get them out of your life completely so you can find peace, calm and self-respect.

If you suspect that your ex is emotionally abusing or manipulating your children it might be an idea to look into family therapy if that is a possibility.

Chapter 9. The Healing Process

"You can't solve a problem by staying in the same energy in which it was created." Albert Einstein.

In my search for who I am I realized that all life is based on energy and vibrations. I had to take on a different vibration, a higher vibration to get me from where I was to where I wanted to go.

There is no one thing I can tell you that will automatically heal your heart and make you feel better. You have to make the first step - it won't just happen. You have to make the decision to feel better by looking on the positive side of life, which raises your vibration.

Negative vibrations are slow and sluggish. Have you ever seen the way a depressed person walks? They walk slowly, their shoulders are hunched, their head is hung and they drag their feet along very slowly. Whereas a person who is feeling great about themselves and about life will walk tall, their head is held up high, they walk with a spring in their step and a smile on their face. Try walking like that, even if you don't feel like it. Taking on the physical actions of a person who feels great, immediately gives you a boost. You'll start feeling better every time you do it. There is a close connection between the mind and the body. So fake it 'till you make it!

LONELINESS

Some awkward moments might come for you at those special days you had with your ex, such as birthdays, Christmas or Valentine's Day. Keep yourself occupied on these days with some sort of a project. You may find yourself upset when you go to a place where you both used to go or something else familiar triggers a memory. If you've been with your ex for a long time you'll probably find that most things remind you of him. If you do find yourself lapsing into daydreams about the so-called good times think of twice as many bad times until you feel lucky that you are out of the relationship. If you need to – keep a list in your handbag of all the bad things he did to you and look at it to bring you back to reality.

Loneliness is a normal part of ending a relationship. Don't expect to feel fine just because you are away from the abuse. You are also away from what is familiar and that may be a little daunting and scary for a while. Keep busy and try to have an active social life with friends and family. Rediscover any old interests that have slipped by the wayside.

We've all heard that time heals all wounds. The fact is that some people take a lot longer than others. If it takes you months or years then that's okay. Don't put any time restrictions on yourself as long as you are improving. After a long period of time has gone by and you feel you aren't improving it may be best to speak to a counselor.

GRIEF

Even though you have left a bad situation it's normal to grieve. You are grieving for the relationship, the partner you once had and you may also be grieving for the person who you used to be.

Psychiatrists have identified various stages of grief, which include denial, anger, depression then lastly, acceptance.

You may not go through all of these stages and you may resolve your grief without going through any of the above stages. There is no typical response to grief.

Grieving is a very real and overwhelmingly strong emotion. You may find yourself unable to cope with day-to-day activities. I found myself unable to work for some time. Fortunately, I found that going back to study helped divert my attention and it kept my mind occupied.

Guilt can be one major factor in grief. If you still have any sort of contact with your ex they will be doing the best they can to make you feel guilty and make you feel that you were in the wrong for leaving.

You may feel confused by your grieving feelings if you were the one who left the relationship. Either way, whether he left or you left, your life has changed and that leads to a process of grieving. Don't expect other people to sympathize with you because they probably aren't going to understand what you are going through. Other people think you should be grateful that you are finally away from the relationship and don't understand why you aren't happy instantly.

When someone's partner dies, the remaining partner gets understanding and sympathy, which helps the griever. You are going through the same pain just as if your partner had died. Your loss and hurt is often felt the same.

Remember, that there is no proper time limit, so don't worry if you are taking a long time to work through the grief. Ignoring grief will do more harm than good. If you try and ignore it it will just keep resurfacing until you deal with it

ANGER:

How could he do this to me? Is he going to get away with it? He's left me with nothing!

In my case I was left with no money so I was very, very angry. This lasted for some time. I would think back to how he cleverly and carefully manipulated my financial situation so that if I left it would be with nothing. I found it hard to comprehend how one human could do that to another especially when that person was professing undying love to me.

When I wasn't thinking about my financial situation, I would think back to something that happened in the relationship and I would feel like phoning him and asking him why he did it or I'd want to try to make him see what he has done to me. Then I realized that he will twist things inside out and the conversation would go nowhere and I know that I will end up angrier and with more frustration. I channel my energy in another direction instead.

There are so many things you could feel angry about. It's normal to feel angry for the way he has treated you. It's also normal to be angry with yourself for letting him do that to you and for not leaving sooner than you did. It's healthy to express the anger and you shouldn't hold it in.

*It helps to write down everything you are angry about.

*Scream (try doing this in the car so the neighbors don't call the police).

* Go for a run or throw yourself in to something.

*After a period of anger, just be resigned to let it go.

*You can't do anything about what happened; you can only control your reaction to what happened to you.

*Try not to dwell on it by thinking of things you should have or could have said or done. It will just keep negativity in your life for longer than it needs to be.

*He'll probably never realize or admit that he did anything wrong so at some point you've just got to be resigned to leave it as some awful thing that happened to you and take what positives you can from it.

DEPRESSION:

You're also probably going to experience some level of depression with varying intensity. Do what you can to alleviate the depression.

*Try natural mood elevators such as exercise and chocolate.
*Watch funny movies and find things to laugh at.
*Surround yourself with positive people.
*Take a walk in nature.
*Appreciate the world you live in.
*Meditation and yoga control stress levels and are mood elevators as well.

FORGIVENESS.

"The weak can never forgive. Forgiveness is the attribute of the strong." - Gandhi

Why should I forgive him for what he's done to me? He's ruined my life!

Forgiveness is not saying that what he did to you is okay. You aren't accepting his behavior at all. You are forgiving him for yourself. It is much easier to give forgiveness than to carry hurt pain and anger within yourself.

You do not have to contact the person who abused you to forgive them. They don't even have to know you have forgiven them.

You can do it within yourself or even create a little ceremony where you imagine that your abuser is there in front of you. Consider these ideas:

Abusers were often abused as children or in a previous relationship. What they did to you wasn't about you; it was about the pain that lives inside them. If you have trouble with forgiving them, but you want to, try seeing them as the child that they used to be.

Forgiveness is making peace for you and letting the pain of it go.

If you aren't ready to forgive or don't want to forgive, the choice is yours. Forgiveness is not necessary to re-program your mind; it's just an option.

THERAPY

I admit that personally, I'm not one for therapy. Having said that I realized that John and I needed help and I asked him to go to therapy many times. He refused saying that we should be able to work out our own problems.

Typically the abuser won't go to therapy, or say they will, but never do. It's difficult for the average therapist to counsel couples who are in an abusive relationship as there are often complex power mechanisms within the relationship. In emotionally abusive relationships, both people in the relationship are not equally at fault. Most therapists are trained to treat people equally even though with the abused couple there is a victim and a perpetrator.

Therapy always sounds good and people think that therapy will work. It works for some people, but many claim that it doesn't work for them.

If the therapist is not familiar with patterns of abuse, the abuser may seem innocent, as their deeds are often invisible whereas the reaction of the upset victim is all too visible. For example, often times the abuser often frustrates the victim so much that she will get angry and upset, whereas the victim will remain as cool as a cucumber.

If you have left the abusive situation you may benefit from going to see a therapist, but that is not the answer for everyone. It also may not even be a possibility for a lot of people.

I went to one session by myself while I was still in the relationship with John. I felt that I wasn't normal because John was always pointing out ways in which I wasn't being 'normal'. The therapist asked me what normal was. That was a good point. What is normal? She confirmed that John was acting in emotionally abusive ways, as I had always suspected.

LOOK FOR THE LESSON – LEARN FROM YOUR EXPERIENCE.

Accept that you've had a bad experience but see it as a positive in your life - not as a negative. They say if you don't learn lessons the first time around the same things happen in your life until you learn what you are meant to learn from the experience. This was true in my case. I had a very abusive first marriage and then a few years later got involved with John. No man attracted me in those three years in between my first husband and John. I often wondered if that was because I was waiting for another abuser.

If nothing else, your abuser has taught you what you do want in a relationship and what you don't want. That's a great start.

Life is about changing and growing. Try not to harbor bitterness or anger for your abuser. That is just bad for your health and well-being. Bitterness and sorrow are negative and will eat away at you.

I put a post-it on my mirror and it was there for a very long time, it read – Thank you helped me create my perfect relationship and I am on my way to it. Yay! Sounds silly? Maybe, but when I got sad I would see that and I would immediately feel better.

See your abuser as a teacher who came to teach you a valuable lesson - to show you a better way of living your life. They have also helped you to know what you want and want you don't want from future relationships.

Life is a learning process, so don't see this relationship as a negative thing in your life. See it as a positive thing and take what you can from it.

What have you learned? You have learned that you are an individual, you matter, and your taste and your opinions are fantastic because they are yours. You will not be a doormat and you will not be molded into a different person. You are unique. You will keep your likes, dislikes and personality just as they are.

Chapter 10. Build your confidence and self-esteem

Take some time out for yourself, to find out what you want for your life. Resist any urge to jump into another relationship. It may be tempting to find someone else to take your mind off your last relationship. That isn't really fair to yourself or the next person you start dating. You need to have a dating detox, take some time for your wounds to heal.

Even if you don't realize it, if you've been in an abusive relationship you will be suffering from a lowered self-esteem. Realize that all the things your partner said about you are not true and they were only said in an effort to manipulate and control you.

HOW DO I LOOK?

Women are put under a lot of pressure to look a certain way. If we don't look like the women in the magazines then most of us feel bad. We are bombarded with advertisements everywhere, for products, which will make us, look younger or get slimmer. The reality of looking like that is that most of us would have to spend all the day in the gym and possibly have to have plastic surgery.

The logical end result of this is that all women would end up looking exactly the same and there would be no individuality. Have you ever noticed that people who have had a lot of work done all look the same? Their noses are the same, their lips are all pumped and their faces are all puffy due to filler.

Don't get me wrong I'm all for surgery if that's what someone wants to do, but I'm more for individuality and personality. That's what makes people unique and different from other people. Who wants to look like other people? A lot of 'before and after' photos I've seen, I actually prefer the before photos. I think people are striving to look different than they are because they think what they are is not good enough and when they change this or that then that will be the answer, and then they will measure up.

Different societies value different looks. Some cultures like voluptuous women and some societies and cultures like women with sagging breasts. The preference for a certain type of look has been programmed into our culture by the media in general.

Some people's self-image is so bad that they just plainly can't see how good they look just the way they are. If you've ever seen the program on television called 'How to Look Good Naked' you would have seen women who think they are unattractive. Gok, the host makes modest changes to their clothing and hair and then other people are asked to comment on how they look. Other people give genuine positive responses. By the end of the program the woman's confidence has improved so much that she poses semi nude for a photographic session. It just shows how much we are influenced by the opinion of others or what we perceive to be others opinions.

I ACCEPT MYSELF

Be happy with how you are and accept yourself exactly how you are right now, whether you are fat, thin or somewhere in between. If you are thin – great! If you are fat – great! Somewhere in between – great! Stop being a slave to someone else's idea of the 'ideal woman'. It's been made up by a man somewhere to make all women miserable and dissatisfied. All people have different tastes so what's the frantic rush for everyone to look like they are starving or to look like a Stepford wife? Cherish your individuality. When you accept yourself you will find that others will reflect that acceptance of yourself.

LOVE YOURSELF

When you were a baby you didn't have any inbuilt preconceptions of yourself - you didn't think you were fat, stupid or ugly. Anything negative we think about ourselves has come from other people's perceptions of us, or the words others have spoken about us.

As we were growing up we mirrored other people's perceptions and took them as our own. *If they think that about me then it must be true. If they say that about it must be true.*

If you weren't bullied or picked on by an older sibling or a parent you may have been teased at school.

I can barely remember one person at school who wasn't picked on in my school days. If you had anything about you that was slightly different then you were a target for teasing, name-calling or getting picked on. I wasn't picked on too badly. I had glasses in those days and glasses weren't cool back then. So I was called 'four eyes.' I didn't mind because I thought I was fat and nobody called me fat, so I was pleased about that. I guess there would have been one or two popular kids who weren't picked on - but hell, the rest of us were.

These taunts from the school years still haunt a lot of people. I have recently heard two people say that it still affects them that they were always picked last to go on the sports teams at school.

These pains are still ingrained and real to many people. The feeling that they were so horrible, so awful that they were picked last which means that everyone else is better than them. How much more awful can things get? To make things even more embarrassing everyone was watching *you* get picked last. That's major rejection going on there.

The results of all those negative feelings combine to give you a self-image. Whether you like it or not how other people see you has influenced the way that you perceive yourself.

MIRROR WORK

Do you have a critical inner voice? Does that voice tell you that you are stupid, silly or dumb? Change your inner critic to a loving and caring voice. Start by praising yourself and telling yourself you are beautiful, clever and wonderful. Do some mirror work where you look in the mirror and tell yourself, 'I love you.' It might feel strange at first, but the stranger it feels the more it will help you. In Louise Hay's book, 'You Can Heal Your Life,' she includes some marvelous exercises, which will help you develop more loving self-talk and improve your self-esteem. Part of self-acceptance is releasing other people's opinions.

Below is an example:

Look in the mirror and say, "I love and approve of myself exactly as I am."

Self-approval and self-acceptances are the keys to positive changes in your life.

TAKE THE FOCUS OFF YOURSELF

Sometimes it helps to take the attention off yourself and your problems and think about other people. Try the following: Three times a day deliberately do or say something nice for someone else. Give a compliment, hold the door open for someone, give a word of praise. Do that and watch the other person's face light up. That's the quickest way to feel good and it also boosts your confidence.

CONFIDENCE BUILDING IDEAS

*Make a list of all the positive things about yourself. Then make another list of everything that you are good at. Make another list of all your achievements. Write down even the smallest of things.

*Never say negative things to yourself, keep yourself talk positive.

*Have you let yourself go? Does your hair need cutting or coloring? Go get it done. If you look good it also helps you feel good.

*Wear perfume even if you don't normally use it. It has a marvelous mood altering effect.

*Make a list of all the things you have been putting off and cross them off as you do them. For example, that trip to the dentist or even cleaning out the bathroom cupboard.

*Don't walk around with chipped nail polish or dirty clothes, the better you look, the better you'll feel.

*Take a look at where you are living. Just by cleaning it from top to bottom and clearing away all the 'clutter' it will also transform your mood. Create airflow and let light in, try some fresh flowers. Buy some white sage, (light it then blow it out so it's smoking) and take it around your house, apartment or room (especially in the corners) and visualize all the negativity flowing out of your place.

* Look after your body by way of eating healthy and getting exercise.

*Find a creative outlet, such as gardening, sketching or writing poetry.

*Get plenty of sleep. If you have trouble sleeping there are excellent recordings with sounds of rain or sounds of the forest that may help you to fall asleep. If that fails, just lie there and relax and try and not think about anything. If you get stressed about not sleeping that only makes things worse.

*Take a class, dancing, yoga, computer skills or anything you've wanted to do but never took the time (or were never 'allowed' to do).

*Get involved with the community and do some volunteer work.

*Avoid people who put you down and make you feel bad about yourself.

*Treat yourself for the improvements you make.

DO FEEL GOOD THINGS

Above all, do things that feel good to you and that make you happy. Go out and get an ice-cream or go to the gym. Put music on that you like to listen to. Whatever makes you feel better. Reconnecting with friends and family will make you feel better about yourself. Or if they are the source of negativity in your life go out and make some new friends. Good ways to make new friends are by meeting people while you are doing things that you like to do. If you don't have any suitable interests or hobbies that involve people go out and take some group lessons in something you'd like to learn about. Remember the person you used to be, remember the goals you used to have. Make some goals and plans, even if they are just little tiny ones.

Chapter 11. Kick start your New Life

The power to have a better life and cut the cycle of abuse is within you.

Before you can heal, your mind has to be reprogrammed. If you have just gotten away from the abuse, your mind will be programmed to think that abuse is your normal way of life.

If you don't change your patterns and your inner world there will be a transmitter on top of your head, and radiating out from it will be a call to all abusers out there to come and find you. Have you ever noticed you end up dating the same type of guys?

If you do nothing there is a good chance you will continue the pattern of abuse and other people will be pulled toward you to vent their abuse on you.

As mentioned previously, it's pretty likely that you have been abused before in one form or another. Loving yourself is vitally important to your quality of life. If you don't love and respect yourself it is too easy to let others abuse you.

It has been proven by quantum physics that thoughts are real things and thoughts can affect our physical world. That is why it is so important to get rid of the anger and frustration as soon as you can and replace them with optimistic thoughts and thoughts of self-acceptance and worthiness.

This may take a while if you have recently left the relationship. Give yourself time to feel the anger, the hurt and the pain. However, when you are ready to improve the quality of your life it's vitally important to start loving, respecting and forgiving yourself.

CHANGE YOUR THOUGHTS

Life is not beyond our control. It is a scientifically proven fact that thoughts and intents can change reality. So it is important that you have good thoughts and positive thoughts. These thoughts will change your outer world and attract good things to you.

Dr. Masaru Emoto made a ground-breaking discovery decades ago, which clearly shows the affect of human consciousness on water molecules. We can understand this better if we can understand that all life forms, including our thoughts; everything in the universe is fundamentally a vibration!

In experiments, Dr. Emoto exposed music, words spoken, words typed, pictures and videos to water. After it was crystallized the water, under high magnification, showed some remarkable patterns. Positive words such as 'Thank You', 'Love', 'Truth', 'Compassion', and 'Happiness' gave the water molecule a beautiful crystalline structure. The water, which was exposed to negative words and intentions, such as 'hate', 'greed', 'you make me sick' made the structure all distorted and chaotic. If you're interested to know more, Dr Emoto's book is called "The Hidden Messages in Water".

If thoughts, feelings and words have the ability to change the structure of atoms, imagine what they can do with everything else. Our thoughts do affect our reality so it's important that our thoughts are positive. Dwell on what you want for your life and imagine it playing out exactly the way you want it to. Those thoughts are vibrations, which are tangible, and they will make a change in your life.

THE LAW OF ATTRACTION – 'Like attracts like.'

A few years ago a movie called 'The Secret' came out, soon after, a book followed. This started the huge 'law of attraction' movement. What has this got to do with abuse? The law of attraction works on the principle of 'like attracts like.'

What you think about, and what you 'feel' is what you attract.

For example, if you are have deep down feelings that you are not worthy of a good relationship, what you will get is exactly what you are feeling which is *not* a good relationship. If you have been in a really bad relationship and your dominant vibration is 'I don't want to get into another bad relationship, I don't want to get into another bad relationship,' What you are most likely to attract is 'another bad relationship' because that is your dominant *feeling*.

Jerry and Esther Hicks have been teaching on the law of attraction for many, many years. I listened to their teachings for hours a day when I escaped my abuser, and they really helped me to get my thinking straight. Esther channels ancient beings, which call themselves 'Abraham'. If you have a problem with the whole concept of channeling, just put that to one side and listen to their teachings. For those who aren't familiar with Abraham Hicks it's the law of attraction message. I can highly recommend any books by Esther Hicks.

In the movie 'The Secret' by Rhonda Byrne they talk of creating a 'vision board.' Find pictures that represent any goals or dreams you have and put them on your vision board. Your higher self, subconscious, the higher power, will immediately be set into motion to source these things and bring them to you. I've heard of many success stories using this method, but the best one is this one: In The Secret movie they give an example of a man who had just moved into a multi-million dollar home. He was unpacking boxes which he hadn't opened for many years. In one of the boxes he found his old vision board. As he was looking at it he realized that the house that he pasted on his vision board all those years ago was the exact same house that he had just moved into.

Turn to whatever spiritual path you follow. Some find peace and comfort in religion. If you don't currently have something like that, then find something that soothes you and comforts you.

Think good things, be happy and good things will come to you.

POSITIVE THOUGHTS

Look on the positive side of everything - this will fast track your recovery.

If you are old enough to remember Pollyanna's glad game that's a good way to stay positive (I guess this was the 1960s version of the law of attraction). Pollyanna saw the good in everything no matter how bad it seemed. She would say, 'I'm glad it's raining because now I can play with my dolls inside.' Instead of being miserable that it was raining.

I'm sure you've heard that the glass can be half full or half empty. You can be sad you've wasted all those years on him or you can say, 'I'm glad I was in that relationship. It's helped me realize what I want and what I don't want in a relationship.' 'It's helped me to find a new direction in my life.' 'My life begins now.'

VISUALIZATION

Science has confirmed the power of visualization. Experiments have been performed on athletes who were visualized playing their sport. It was found that the brain cannot tell the difference between actually performing an act and imagining that same act. The same areas of the brain are activated.

Visualize what you want to happen for your life. More important than the visualization is the 'feeling' that goes along with the visualization. Have a good 'feeling' about whatever it is that you want to happen.

Visualizing is a way of programming your subconscious mind to help us get thing things we are visualizing. When we continue to visualize day by day, our mind becomes uncomfortable because we are thinking something different to what our reality is, so our mind finds ways to make what we are visualizing become our reality. This may occur by us suddenly having a bright idea about something, or we will suddenly realize we should be doing something a different way. Or it will attract to us people, circumstances or events to help us attain the goal.

Jack Canfield, before he was a famous author, visualized a goal of $100,000 and set a time limit of one year in which to earn it. It took a few weeks then ideas started to come to him. He got an idea to send a book he had written some years ago to a publisher. That book was called 'Chicken Soup for the Soul.' He received an advance from the publisher for just under $100,000 and it was in less than one year, just as he had visualized. That book has been on the best-seller lists for many years.

A good book on visualization is 'Excuse me Your Life is Waiting' by Lynn Grabhorn it is an old book, but a very good one. Lynn speaks of her own life experiences and how she visualized her way to having what she wanted.

MEDITATION

Focus on the inner you. Meditation is deeply relaxing for your mind and sharpens your thinking. According to Deepak Chopra levels of cortisol and adrenaline (these things control stress levels) are lower in the bodies of long term meditators, and their coping mechanisms are better than average.

Many have tried meditation and have given up because they 'can't do it'. What they don't realize is that the very thing that they are doing, that is 'trying to do it' *is* meditation. It is only natural that thoughts will come to you, or that your inner voice will keep speaking to you. Don't get agitated when this happens, just know that it is normal and let the voice go and simply let any thoughts glide right by you. In letting thoughts drift by and not entertaining them you are training your mind. This is in itself a form of meditation.

When you meditate it is best to sit down and keep your back straight. If you lie down you might fall asleep.

You can find meditation music on YouTube or through Google. Or just put some soft music on. You may want to start with about five minutes. Use a timer so you won't have to keep checking the time.

Empty your mind of thoughts and let yourself go. You may feel a sense of release because you don't have to think of anything. If you keep getting distracted by thoughts concentrate on your breathing, in for four and out for four. You may like to try with your eyes open and focus on a flickering candle flame.

Another technique you may like to try is to bring your awareness into your body. Be aware of the aliveness of your body, down through your feet and your toes and feel the aliveness of yourself right though out your body.

Try and meditate every day even if it is just five minutes a day and try and work up to twenty minutes twice a day. I know you're thinking, 'Woaahh, I don't have the time for that!' Take it out of your sleeping time. You won't notice it and you'll sleep more soundly as well.

You will most likely find that once you start meditating you will be able to think more clearly and often good ideas about things and solutions to problems will present themselves.

KEEP A JOURNAL

People have experienced positive changes in their lives by keeping a gratitude journal and writing in it every day, about the things they are grateful for. If you are depressed and feel you don't have anything to be grateful for then start with small things that you probably haven't even noticed. Do you have a warm bed, a roof over your head, enough to eat, your health, people who care for you? Whenever you are feeling a little bit down writing down what you are grateful for will immediately lift you up and change your vibration.

Write down 'feel good' things about yourself and really 'feel' that they are true.

I am beautiful, I am successful, I have good friends, I work with great people, and everything I do is prosperous. Whatever you want to happen for you in your life - write it down.

Make up your own lists of positive affirmations and write them every morning over breakfast. Some people recommend saying their affirmations, but I find if I write them down they get into my subconscious further.

What is an affirmation? Affirmations are phrases, which are stated, in the positive sense.

For example:

I am fit and I am healthy

Good things always come to me

I am a prosperity magnet

Positive people surround me

I am successful at work

I love the work I do

Chapter 12. Dating after abuse – avoid the pitfalls

If you've read the book up until now you should be able to recognize and understand what emotional abuse is. If you don't recognize it and know how to deal with it then you are at risk of continually suffering from it. Before entering into another relationship you need to be fully healed from your previous relationship. You need to realize how you played a part in allowing your partner to treat you the way he did.

Go slowly with the next relationship. Don't be paranoid, but be aware of the warning signs so you don't repeat past patterns. People who have been abused often end up with another abuser – make sure you aren't one of those people.

Think back over your last relationship and think of all the things you could or should have done differently. Would you do the same things in the same way? Think back to when he was being critical of you - what would you say now?

Hindsight is a good thing and it's not very easy to think clearly when you are confronted with something that you don't expect.

WHAT HAPPENED AT THE BEGINNING?

Think back to the beginning of the abusive relationship and ask yourself the following questions. Better to do this with pen and paper so you can see it in black and white.

*When did you notice the first signs that something was wrong?

*When the above event first happened what did you do about it?

*What would you do about if it happens in your next relationship?

*What have you learned from it?

Let's go through this step-by-step.

What was the first sign? Let's say it was that he complained about what you were wearing. What did you do about it? You probably felt really bad and changed into something that would make him happy. Right?

What would you do if that happened in your next relationship? You'd probably state in an emphatic manner, "Look, honey I appreciate your comments, but I really like this and I feel good in it so I'm going to wear it."

* * *

Dr Phil says that people teach you how to treat them. In what ways were you giving him the message that it was all right to abuse you? Did you ever stand up for yourself? Maybe you did and got 'punished' for doing so, but if you stayed in the relationship you were showing him that there were absolutely no consequences for his behavior towards you. Essentially he 'got away' with his bad behavior even to the point where you were reinforcing that this pattern of abuse was working for him. His behavior was giving him something that he needed which was the power and the control in the relationship. You were the object of his control.

If you are still in an abusive relationship stop and think – Is this really the type of person you want in your life? People who use emotional abuse can change, but they can only change if they acknowledge that they have a problem. Only you can decide whether you want to continue to put yourself at risk of abuse or whether you want to have a quieter life without all the drama that goes along with being in one of these relationships.

It's a lot of work to keep enforcing your boundaries after the pattern of abuse has already been established and become a regular pattern in someone's life. Can you keep putting in the effort that is required? Can you keep feeling bad about yourself while you hope that this person will improve?

For me the answer was no. I reached a point where I had almost totally lost my identity. My life was revolving around what he wanted and I continually strove to feel 'good enough.' I took a good hard think about how I liked to feel. I realized that the major thing I wanted out of life to have calmness, serenity and peace. I knew I couldn't have that and also have a relationship with John.

Like a lot of other women I had became too much of a *doormat* in my eagerness to please. What I wanted and needed out of life had ceased to be important as long as he was happy. The thing is – he *never was* happy!

Don't buy into the Cinderella story and try and make the relationship work at the cost of your own well being.

Everyone loves love. It's great to be in love and have that warm fuzzy feeling about someone and the butterflies in the stomach. Sometimes though, these feelings make us jump too quickly into a relationship and ignore the little warning signs that all isn't well. Let's face it, it's an effort to go out and find someone else and then you have to get to know them. It was hard enough finding this – or what you thought was a - half reasonable toad, so you want to try and make this one work.

At the end of the day it is you who are responsible for your own well-being. Guard that responsibility and put your own needs first. Don't lose who you are and what you want, to please a man. Keep sight of your goals and know what you want from life. Don't forget that you are a person too.

Of course there is give and take in all relationships just be aware of keeping the balance.

Set your boundaries at the first sign of any abuse. In Chapter 11, I have a list of boundaries, which you can base your own list of boundaries on.

Remember that you deserve love and you deserve to be in a loving, caring and safe relationship.

CHANGE YOUR OLD PATTERNS:

Try some of these changes.

* If you really like a guy after the first date, try waiting a while before going out on the next date; alternatively keep seeing other people as well. It's important to not get too carried away by a guy at the initial dating stage – keep your thinking straight.

*Don't have sex with someone straight away. This is a big no no if you are looking for a permanent relationship. Particularly for *you,* since you've been in an abusive relationship in the past. It's simply that sex clouds your judgment and you don't think with your head, you start thinking with a lower part of your anatomy. You won't be able to see his faults and a part of you will feel emotionally committed to him before your head tells you you're allowed to be committed. You don't know him yet so you don't know if he is worthy of you.

*Start doing things you enjoy on your own. It's important to be happy with and enjoy your own company.

*If you do start dating the person more frequently don't start obsessing over them. E.g. what are they doing, what are they thinking, where are they right now. This is normal if you like someone however, you have to be careful since you've been in a bad relationship once before. You have to be careful that you remain the most important person and that you never put yourself or leave yourself in harm's way again. It's more important to keep the focus on you -what are you thinking right now, what are you doing?

* * *

As you can see, I like to use a lot of lists. They are very helpful in organizing your thoughts and to clarify your feelings.

Be very clear in what you want in another relationship. Typically, if you were in a bad relationship you let them get away with their behavior by not standing up to them. This time you will have to be firm with this and think with your head and not your heart. Thinking with your heart and making excuses is what caused you to stay with the abuser.

Obviously, don't jump into a new relationship straight away; give yourself plenty of healing time.

When you do start dating again, just relax. It may be tough to start with because you will be looking for the warning signs in case he is another abuser. It's a fine line to tread too – you want to see the best in everyone, but at the same time you must also be aware whether abuse is rearing its ugly head. That's why it's a good idea to take things very slowly.

If you do see signs of abusive behavior towards you, and they haven't listened to you regarding their behavior, then it is time to move on. It's much easier to leave at the start of the relationship before your lives and finances become entangled.

Now grab your journal.

I recommend you make the following lists.

WHAT MY IDEAL PARTNER LOOKS LIKE –

I don't mean just looks, I'm talking about every aspect of your new partner, personality, emotional values, spiritual values, temperament.

MY IDEAL PARTNER

Has a sense of humor

Is kind, caring and affectionate

Intelligent

Is easy to talk to and communicate with

Sexually compatible

Lets me do my own thing

Displays socially acceptable behavior

Respects me and other people

Encourages me in all things

Lets me have my privacy

Trusts me in all things

(Continue to add your own wants and likes stated in a positive sense)

* * *

To take this step further and really visualize this person by:

Take a sheet of paper and right down what your ideal partner looks like. And I don't mean in just a physical way. I mean emotionally and personality wise. What type of personality suits you best? Intelligent, caring, funny?

Here are some questions to help clarify the type of person you want.

How does he react when you are crying?

How does he react when you are sad?

How does he react when you really want to talk about something with him?

How does he react when you tell him he hurt or upset you over something?

How does he react when you tell him you want to go away on a girls' weekend?

How does he react if you get a big promotion or find success in a venture?

How does he react if it's your turn to cook and you just don't feel like it?

THIS IS MY RELATIONSHIP BILL OF RIGHTS – These are all the things I am entitled to within a loving and caring relationship.

Relationship Bill of Rights

I have the right to:

An equal and healthy relationship with my partner

Be respected

Change my mind

Kindness from my partner

Emotional support

Be listened to politely by my partner

Have my own opinions even if my partner disagrees

Have my own feelings

Be angry with someone I love

Clear and honest answers to questions that concern me

Live free from accusation and blame

Express all my feelings

Live free from criticism and judgment

Have my work and interests spoken of with respect

Encouragement

Live free from emotional and physical threat

Live free from angry outburst and rage

Be called by no name that hurts, or puts me down

Be respectfully asked rather than ordered

Be myself as long as I am respectful of others

Not have physical or sexual contact with my partner when I choose

Adapted from the Domestic Violence and Sexual Assault Coalition

DEAL-BREAKERS / BOUNDARIES

Make a list of your deal-breakers or boundaries. These are behaviors that you definitely will not and cannot tolerate. Also, once someone exhibits a deal breaking behavior what are you going to do about it? You have to be prepared to walk away. Alternatively give one warning and then walk away.

DEAL-BREAKERS – BOUNDARIES List

I will not tolerate any of the following behaviors:

Swearing at me

Calling me hurtful names

Being unreasonably suspicious or jealous

Checking up on me

Lying to me

Screaming at me

The silent treatment

Withdrawal of affection

Infidelity

Shoving me, pushing me or any negative physical contact

Demeaning me

WHAT DOES A HEALTHY RELATIONSHIP LOOK LIKE?

One very important thing: You may really like a man and he really likes you and everything is going along great, but you feel that something is 'missing.' Could it be the thing that is 'missing' is that he isn't abusing you and it feels foreign? You have no push pull going on with your heart? Don't let a fantastic man who you love go because he isn't pulling on your heart and 'playing' you emotionally.

If you are anything like me you've forgotten what a healthy relationship looks like and wonder if you've ever actually been in one. We all know relationships are about compromise and they aren't rosy a hundred percent of the time.

Healthy relationships are built on mutual respect, trust and open communication.

HEALTHY RELATIONSHIP

Below is a scenario of a healthy relationship

The individuality of both partners remains intact

There is equality

You feel safe

There is mutual acceptance

You are free to express your opinion even though it could be contrary to your partner's opinion

You feel free to ask for what you want and need

There is mutual respect

Both partners have boundaries

Both partners are honest

Both partners make the relationship a priority over other things

There is no abuse

Perfection is not expected. We are all human and we are all going to make mistakes

You are free to grow as an individual

Each partner is responsible for themselves

You solve any problems together

There is open communication on all subjects

You remain an individual and don't lose your identity
Both parties feel free to negotiate any issues
You feel free to be yourself

Chapter 13. What the Research says about Emotional Abuse.

A lot of emotional abuse goes unreported for various reasons such as shame, embarrassment or isolation. So we can assume that the figures for emotional abuse are much higher than stated. Below are Australian statistics, which are similar to other western countries.

According to the Centers for Disease Control and Prevention, physical violence is most typically accompanied by emotional or psychological abuse. Inter personal violence whether it is physical, psychological or sexual can lead to psychological consequences such as:

Anxiety

Depression

Symptoms of post-traumatic stress disorder (PTSD)

Antisocial behavior

Suicidal behavior in females

Low self-esteem

Inability to trust others, especially in intimate relationships
Fear of intimacy
Emotional detachment
Sleep disturbances
Flashbacks
Replaying assault in the mind

In 1996, the National Clearinghouse on Family Violence, for Health Canada, reported that 39% of married women or common-law wives suffered emotional abuse by husbands/partners. The statistics for men experiencing emotional abuse by women were not addressed by this study.

These statistics come from the Australian Bureau of Statistics Personal Safety Survey (2006), which is the largest and most recent survey of violence in Australia. These are the findings:
29.8% victims of current partner violence since the age of 15 were male
24.4% victims of previous partner violence since the age of 15 were male

29.4% victims of sexual assault* during the last 12 months were male

26.1% victims of sexual abuse* before the age of 15 were male

The SA Interpersonal Violence and Abuse Survey (1999) found that:

32.3% victims of reported domestic violence by a current or ex-partner (including both physical and emotional violence and abuse) were male

19.3% victims of attempted or actual forced sexual activity since they turned 18 years of age were male (excluding activity from partners or ex-partners). Both this survey and the Personal Safety Survey excluded the male prison population where over one quarter of young inmates experience sexual assault.

DID YOU SUFFER EMOTIONAL ABUSE AS A CHILD?

In an article on USAToday.com, Dec. 17, 2010: According to the U.S. Centers for Disease Control and Prevention (CDC) almost 60% of American adults reported difficult childhoods involving abusive and troubled family members or absent parents due to separation or divorce. 9% of those surveyed reported that they underwent five or more 'adverse childhood experiences' such as verbal, physical or sexual abuse.

According to the NSPCC in the UK (The NSPCC was founded in 1884 and their vision is to end cruelty to children in the UK) all forms of abuse and neglect include an element of emotional abuse and it is for this reason that emotional abuse has often been overlooked as an obstacle for children to live a happy and healthy life.

Whether on its own or whether emotional abuse is coupled with other forms of abuse, it can have a serious long-term affect on a child's emotional development and health.

Emotional abuse is the second most common reason for being made subject to a child protection plan or to put the child on the child protection register in England, Wales and Scotland.

Emotional abuse is often linked or is the forerunner to other forms of abuse. The parents of emotionally abused children have often experienced abuse themselves as a child. Stress is often linked to emotional abuse.

The HM Government, 2013 defined emotional abuse as: "The persistent emotional maltreatment of a child such as to cause severe and persistent adverse effects on the child's emotional development. It may involve conveying to a child that they are worthless or unloved, inadequate, or valued only insofar as they meet the needs of another person.

It may also include not giving the child opportunities to express their views, deliberately silencing them or 'making fun' of what they say or how they communicate. It may feature age or developmentally inappropriate expectations being imposed on children. These may include interactions that are beyond a child's developmental capability, as well as over-protection and limitation of exploration and learning, or preventing the child from participating in normal social interaction.

It may involve seeing or hearing the ill-treatment of another. It may involve serious bullying (including cyber-bullying), causing children frequently to feel frightened or in danger, or the exploitation or corruption of children. Some level of emotional abuse is involved in all types of maltreatment of a child, though it may occur alone."

The NSCC recognizes two different types of emotional abuse towards children, which is active emotional abuse, and passive emotional abuse.

Active emotional abuse

"Emotional abuse where someone intentionally tries to scare, demeanor generally verbally abuse a child is known as "active" abuse as it requires a premeditated intention to harm that child." Things included in these behaviors are spurning, terrorizing, isolating, corrupting or even ignoring.

Passive emotional abuse

"Emotional abuse where a parent or carer denies their child the love and care they need in order to be healthy and happy. This can be more difficult to identify because it stems from a carer's lack of care, knowledge or understanding about a child's needs. It is here that the definitions for passive emotional abuse and emotional neglect are very similar."

In passive emotional abuse the parent is not connected and cannot give the love a child needs. The carer/parent has a negative attitude such as having a low opinion of the child and not offering praise or encouragement. They may expect the child to perform tasks, which are way too advanced for their current capabilities. The carer/parent fails to provide adequate socialization for the child.

According to the NSCC – "In 2012 emotional abuse was the most common concern identified at case conferences in Scotland. For England and Wales, emotional abuse was the second most common reason for a child to be placed on the child protection register or made the subject of a child protection plan. The proportion of children subject to a child protection plan or on the child protection register in England and Wales at 31 March 2012 was 28% for emotional abuse. The figures in Northern Ireland were lower at around 13%. This could be because of differences in recording or the small numbers of children on the child protection register in general."

Chapter 14. Conclusion.

Thank you for staying with me until the end of this book. I know I've called you a victim all the way through this book, but you only *stay* a victim as long as you let him continue to bring you down and if you continually dwell on what happened to you. Don't let him continue to ruin and control any aspect of your life any longer. Turn the events of the past into a positive thing and shake off any mentality of being a victim. Mentally thank him for helping you find the real you and setting you on a different and better path.

You should know what emotional abuse looks like if you've read all or most of this book. You've probably identified with the many stories of abuse within these pages.

Leaving the abusive relationship is the beginning not the end. It's the beginning of your road back to peace and the road back to yourself.

Hopefully you have asked yourself some questions and examined the relationship to find out why you let him treat you that way.

Work on healing yourself daily, physically, spiritually and mentally, little by little, keep going forward and gaining self-respect and confidence daily.

Before this book ends just one more WARNING - Warning Bells:

If you feel like you want to go back to your ex and you're having a hard time letting go, realize you aren't alone. Leaving is hard for anyone. Going back is a common phenomenon amongst people who have been the victim of abuse. Goodness knows I did it myself more times than I can count. I think one time I even took him back because I felt sorry for him. Don't forget they are manipulators! They play on your weak points!

If you feel like going back you could be remembering the relationship with a distorted sense of reality and only remembering the goods parts.

Grab a bit of paper and write a list of all the things he did to you, all the ways he hurt, ridiculed and made you feel worthless.

I'll share my 'John' list with you. Then you write your own.

My list of what he did to me.

Told me he thought I was dumb

Nothing I did was good enough

I was scared of his moods

I was scared of his drinking

He didn't like me speaking to my family

He was rude to my friends

He was controlling me in my choice of clothing

He wanted me to wear my hair a certain way

He read my emails and used to go through my phone

He wanted my passwords to social media

He was over jealous without any reason to be

He always had to know where I was

He was inconsistent

He was unpredictable with his temper

He was nasty
He would insult me
He had 'ideals' in his mind, which I had to live up to
Nothing I did ever met with his approval

When you're finished, sit and look at the list and ask yourself – Do you really want to be in a relationship with someone who would treat you like this? You deserve the best. Is this the best? Is this your ideal scenario for your life? Do you want to spend the rest of your life feeling bad about yourself with that horrible feeling in the pit of your stomach?

If that doesn't help go back to Chapter 7. and realize your have gone in to survival mode and are most likely experiencing trauma bonding which distorts rational thinking.

Realize that you are worthy of having a great relationship.
Remember:
To raise your vibration.

Think positively.

You deserve the best partner in the world for you.

You are worth it.

You are worthwhile.

You are special and unique.

You are loveable.

You are loved.

Above all **DO NOT DWELL** on what happened. Replace those thoughts with positive thoughts of what **YOU** want out of life. Visualize and expect a better brighter future! **You deserve it!**

Look forward to good times.

Enjoy!

* * * The End * * *

Contact the author at: bristamara@gmail.com

Or via twitter at http://www.twitter.com/BrisTamara

If you have found this book helpful please leave a review from your place of purchase!

WHERE TO GET HELP: If you are experiencing emotional abuse here are some contact details.

In the US: Call the National Domestic Violence Hotline at **1-800-799-7233**

U.S. and Canada: Call **1-888-7HELPLINE** http://www.dahmw.org This is a Domestic Abuse Helpline for men and women.

In the UK: Call Women's Aid at **0808 2000 247**

For men in the UK: Call **01823 334244**

http://www.mankind.org.uk

Australia: call **1800RESPECT** at **1800 737 732**

Lifeline phone Call **131 114** or live chat at www.lifeline.org.au

Kids Helpline ages 5-25 Call **1800 55 1800**

Suicide Call Back Service Call **1300 65 94 67**

www.suicidecallbackservice.org.au

Worldwide: visit http://www.hotpeachpages.net This is a global directory of helplines and crisis centers.

RECOMMENDED READING:

You Can Heal Your Life by Louise Hay

Ageless Body, Timeless Mind by Deepak Chopra

You Can Create An Exceptional Life by Louise Hay

Ask And It Is Given by Esther Hicks

The Vortex by Esther Hicks

The Astonishing Power of Emotions by Esther Hicks

The Hidden Messages In Water by Masaru Emoto

The Miracle Of Water by Masaru Emoto

Excuse Me Your Life Is Waiting by Lynn Grabhorn

Transcendental Meditation by Mahesh Yogi

Science Of Being And Art Of Living by Maharishi Mahesh Yogi

The Power of Now by Eckhart Tolle

REFERENCES

Chapter 1.

Thompson, AE and CA, Kaplan. 1996. "Childhood emotional abuse." *British Journal of Psychiatry.* 168(2):143-8.

Chapter 4.

Vaknin, Sam. 2007. *The Mind of The Abuser.* Narcissus Publications.

Linehan, Marsha. 1993. Cognitive-behavioral treatment of borderline personality disorder. Guildford Press, New York.

Chapter 7.

Bessell A van der Kolk, MD. 1989. "The Compulsion to Repeat the Trauma." *Psychiatric Clinics of North America.* 12, (2), p 389- 411.

Donald G. Dutton and Susan Painter, 1993. "Emotional Attachment in Abusive Relationships: A Test of Traumatic Bonding." *Violence and Victims.* 8 (2).

Fitzpatrick, Laura. 2009. *"Stockholm Syndrome" Time* 'Understanding Stockholm Syndrome'(pdf, page 10), Federal Bureau of Investigation (FBI).

Carver, Joseph M. 2011. *"Love and Stockholm Syndrome: The Mystery of Loving an Abuser." http://counsellingresource.com/lib/therapy/self-help/stockholm/2/.*

Fuselier, Dwayne G. 1999."Placing the Stockholm Syndrome in Perspective". *FBI Law Enforcement Bulletin*, pp. 22–25.

Dutton, D.G and S.L. Painter. 1981 Traumatic Bonding: the development of emotional attachments in battered women and other relationships of intermittent abuse. *Victimology: An International Journal,* 1(4), pp. 139–155.

Goldner, Virginia. 2004. "When Love Hurts: Treating Abusive Relationships."
Psychoanalytic Inquiry *24.3 pp. 346-372.*

Emoto, Musaru. 2005. *The Hidden Messages in Water*, Beyond Words Publishing, Oregon.

Chapter 9.

Hay, Louise, 2004, *You Can Heal Your Life,* Hay House, New York.

Chapter 10.

Canfield, Jack, 2012. *Chicken Soup for the Soul,* Backlist.

Grabhorn, Lynn, 2000, *Excuse Me Your Life is Waiting,* Hampton Roads Publishing Company, Charlottesville.

Chopra, Deepak, 1988, *Ageless Body, Timeless Mind*, Ebury Press, Rider.

Chapter 12.

Reinberg, Steven. 2010. *CDC: Majority of U.S. Adults had Troubled Childhoods.* http://www.usatoday.com/yourlife/parenting-family/2010-12-17-adult- majority-troubled-childhood_N.htm.

Australian Bureau of Statistics. 2006. *Personal Safety Survey,* Australia, 2005 (reissue), cat. no. 4906.0, ABS, Canberra.

S.A. Department of Human Services. *Interpersonal Violence and Abuse Survey,* 1999,

http://health.adelaide.edu.au/pros/docs/reports/general/violence_interpersonal_violence_survey.pdf.

Tjaden P and N. Thoennes. 2000. *Extent, nature, and consequences of intimate partner violence*: findings from the National Violence Against Women Survey. Washington (DC): Department of Justice (US); Publication No. NCJ 181867. Available from: http://www.ojp.usdoj.gov/nij/pubssum/181867.htm.

Black, M.C. 2011. Intimate partner violence and adverse health consequences: implications for clinicians. *Am J Lifestyle Med* 5(5):428-439.

Center for Disease Control and Prevention http://www.cdc.gov/violenceprevention/intimatepartnerviolence/consequences.html.

BIBLIOGRAPHY

Australian Bureau of Statistics. 2006. *Personal Safety Survey,* Australia, 2005 (reissue), cat. no. 4906.0, ABS, Canberra.

Bessell A van der Kolk, MD. 1989. "The Compulsion to Repeat the Trauma." *Psychiatric Clinics of North America.* 12, (2), p 389- 411.

Black, M.C. Intimate partner violence and adverse health consequences: implications for clinicians. *Am J Lifestyle Med* (2011). 5(5):428-439.

Canfield, Jack, 2012. *Chicken Soup for the Soul.* Backlist.

Carver, Joseph M. 2011. *"Love and Stockholm Syndrome: The Mystery of Loving an Abuser." http://counsellingresource.com/lib/therapy/self-help/stockholm/2/.*

Center for Disease Control and Prevention http://www.cdc.gov/violenceprevention/intimatepartnerviolence/consequences.html.

Chopra, Deepak, 1988, *Ageless Body, Timeless Mind*, Ebury Press, Rider.

Dutton, Donald G. and Susan Painter. 1993. "Emotional Attachment in Abusive Relationships: A Test of Traumatic Bonding," *Violence and Victims*, 8 (2).

Diagnostic and Statistical Manual of Mental Disorders (DSM V).

Emoto, Masuru. *The Hidden Messages in Water*, Beyond Words Publishing, Oregon.

Fuselier, Dwayne. G. 1999. "Placing the Stockholm Syndrome in Perspective". *FBI Law Enforcement Bulletin*, 22–25.

Fitzpatrick, Laura. 2009. *"*Stockholm Syndrome." *Understanding Stockholm Syndrome'* (pdf, page 10), Federal Bureau of Investigation. (FBI).

Goldner, Virginia. 2004. "When Love Hurts: Treating Abusive Relationships." *Psychoanalytic Inquiry* 24.3 (2004), pp. 346-372.

Grabhorn, Lynn, 2000, *Excuse Me Your Life is Waiting,* Hampton Roads Publishing.

Hay, Louise, 2004. *You Can Heal Your Life*, Hay House, New York.

Hay, Louise. 2013. *You Can Create An Exceptional Life*, Hay House, New York.

Hicks, Esther, *Ask and It is Given,* Hay House, New York.

Linehan, Marsha. 1993. *Cognitive-behavioral Treatment of Borderline Personality Disorder*. New York: Guilford Press.

Reinberg, Steven. *CDC: Majority of U.S. Adults had Troubled Childhoods.*

http://www.usatoday.com/yourlife/parenting-family/2010-12-17-adult- majority-troubled-childhood_N.htm. 2010, 17th December, 2010.

S.A. Department of Human Services. 1999. *Interpersonal Violence and Abuse Survey.* http://health.adelaide.edu.au/pros/docs/reports/general/violence_interpersonal_violence_survey.pdf.

Thompson AE and CA Kaplan. 1996. "Childhood emotional abuse." *British Journal of Psychiatry.* 168(2):143-8.

Tjaden P and N Thoennes. 2000. "Extent, nature, and consequences of intimate partner violence:" findings from the National Violence Against Women Survey. Washington (DC): Department of Justice (US); 2000. Publication No. NCJ 181867. Available from: http://www.ojp.usdoj.gov/nij/pubssum/181867.htm.

Vaknin, Sam. 2007. *The Mind of The Abuser* . Narcissus Publications.